IGNITE

Sonja Corbitt and
Deacon Harold Burke-Sivers

Ignite

READ THE BIBLE
LIKE NEVER BEFORE

servant
AN IMPRINT OF
FRANCISCAN MEDIA
Cincinnati, Ohio

Nihil Obstat: Rev. Juntin N. Raines, STL

RESCRIPT
In accord with the Code of Canon Law, I hereby grant my permission to
publish *Ignite*, by Sonja Corbitt and Deacon Harold Burke-Sivers.
Most Reverend David R. Choby
Bishop of the Diocese of Nashville
Nashville, Tennessee
April 4, 2017

Cover design by LUCAS ART AND DESIGN
Book design by Mark Sullivan

Library of Congress Cataloging-in-Publication Data
Names: Corbitt, Sonja, author.
Title: Ignite : read the Bible like never before / Sonja Corbitt and Deacon
Harold Burke-Sivers.
Description: Cincinnati : Servant, 2017.
Identifiers: LCCN 2017025599 | ISBN 9781632531896 (trade paper)
Subjects: LCSH: Bible—Introductions. | Catholic Church—Doctrines.
Classification: LCC BS475.3 .C665 2017 | DDC 220.6/1—dc23
LC record available at https://lccn.loc.gov/2017025599

ISBN 978-1-63253-189-6
Copyright ©2017, Sonja Corbitt and Deacon Harold Burke-Sivers.
All rights reserved.

Published by Servant, an imprint of
Franciscan Media
28 W. Liberty St.
Cincinnati, OH 45202
www.FranciscanMedia.org

Printed in the United States of America.
Printed on acid-free paper.
17 18 19 20 21 5 4 3 2 1

To my mother, Eleanor P. Sivers

(1934 – 2009)

contents

introduction

In our travels and interactions, we often hear that the Bible, the Catholic Church, and Catholic faith feel painfully disconnected from real life. Parents wonder why their kids no longer practice the faith despite weekly Mass attendance, years of Catholic school, and having received confirmation and the other sacraments. Often Catholicism seems like a long list of rules or a dry routine rather than the vibrant life with God it's meant to be. What has caused this widespread disconnect?

"Ignorance of the Scriptures is ignorance of Christ," as St. Jerome said.[1] Simply put, many Catholics don't know Jesus intimately. They have not responded to his invitation to personal, loving, and life-giving communion through the Scriptures.

Yet Deacon Harold and I see regularly how hungry Catholics are for the Bible. They want to know how to study and read this glorious book, but are frequently intimidated by the dryness, length, or difficulty of the study resources available. They often have no idea where to begin with the Bible.

The goal of the *Ignite* study is to give you a starting place in the Scriptures that will allow Jesus to speak directly to your heart through his word. We present the richness and beauty of the Bible in a way that directly connects the incredible story of God's love to your everyday lived experience.

I (Sonja) have often said that if my house burned down, the only possessions, strictly speaking, I would do everything necessary to take with me would be our legal papers and my Bible. Its onionskin pages are so worn and battered that there are many pages taped into it to keep them from falling out. It's heavily marked up and high-lighted, and the pages slide open easily from use. I can locate many of the passages by simply seeing how they look on the page. My Bible is an old friend.

What about yours? If it's not already within reach, locate your Bible, pick it up, and hold it in your hands. Thumb through its pages for a moment or two. Can you locate the Old and New Testaments? Skim through the table of contents. What are your impressions?

Thinking back over your life, try to describe your relationship with the Scriptures in one word. What, if anything, bothers you most about the Bible? What makes you most uncomfortable about it? How do you hope or anticipate your relationship with the Scriptures to change as you work through this study?

Through this series, Deacon Harold and I want the pages of the Bible to enkindle your heart and draw you more deeply into the sacramental life. Our ongoing prayer for you is that *Ignite* will help guide and equip you to experience the depth of God's love so that the Word becomes a living flame in your heart and life.

Whether you participate in a group or alone, throughout your *Ignite* study, we have included special areas to help you connect with God through the Bible. Expect each chapter to include:

—*A Review.* Repetition is the mother of learning, as they say, so we spend a little time revisiting each chapter in a concise way.

—*An Invitation.* This section applies the Scriptures and the chapter to our own lives.

—*A Good Prompt.* Here we offer a LOVE the Word meditation, a handy way to practice getting in touch with God in the Bible, directly and personally.

We used the RSV-CE translation of the Bible for this series. If you are participating in *Ignite* as a group, please be aware that several different versions of the Bible will likely be in use by the participants. Comparing different versions is an important tool in understanding the Bible. Comparing word choices in different translations allows for a more complete picture of what each verse or group of verses means.

Within the silent pages of the ancient book called the Bible, the Spirit of God breathes. He has waited millennia for you there. Because the Bible is a breathtaking love letter from God, he will reveal himself directly to you. What glories will he whisper in your ear? What discoveries will make your heart pound and your spirit soar? If you are ready, let's find out!

chapter one

Lectio Divina, Hearing God Speak

As I (Deacon Harold) finished the final, sending forth address at a diocesan youth conference, I noticed a young man enter the venue near the end of the talk. He was dressed in a delivery uniform and was scanning the crowd, looking for someone. Upon finishing my talk and leaving the stage, the young man quickly approached me. He was very excited and said, "Your story really touched me. I've never heard anyone talk about their faith like that before. Tell me about Jesus!" The young man and I sat down in the back of the arena, and he told me his story.

He explained that he was not a person of faith: he was neither baptized nor ever went to church. His father abandoned the family when he was boy. As a teenager, he decided to track down his dad and discovered that he had committed suicide. The young man had a girlfriend who was Catholic (the person he was looking for earlier) and she was continually trying to convert him by giving him Catholic catechisms, books, and CDs. What she had not explained to him, however, was that it was possible to have an intimate relationship with Jesus. He said that my story moved him deeply and he wanted that same experience of God in his life. I saw that he was hungry for truth—in the person of the Lord Jesus!

His enthusiasm was contagious. He wanted to dive right in and knew that the Bible was important. I happened to have an extra Bible in my bag, but it wasn't just any Bible: it was the Bible that belonged to my mother, who recently passed away. That Bible meant a lot to me, but I knew it would also mean a lot to that young man who was looking for God.

As I handed the Bible to him I told him not to start from the beginning, because by the time he reached the middle of Leviticus he would be scratching his head wondering what was going on. Instead, I encouraged him to start with the Gospels: Matthew, Mark, Luke, and John. I wanted the young man to get to know Jesus personally through the accounts of his life, death, and resurrection.

I told him that each Gospel writer wrote the truth about Jesus, and was addressing his account of Jesus's life to a specific audience. Matthew wrote to the Jews, so he started off with a genealogy to show that Jesus, as the Messiah, was a descendant of Abraham through David. Mark was writing to the first Christians, who were facing persecution. Luke wrote to the Gentiles. John, whose Gospel was the last to be written, wrote for the entire Church, focusing heavily on the divinity of Christ. I mentioned all of this so my young friend would not be confused when, for example, one writer goes into detail about a miracle Christ worked, while another mentions the same miracle only in passing, while another doesn't talk about the miracle at all.

I explained it to him this way. Say you and I went to an event honoring someone special who is important to both of us. If we were to write honestly about the event and our experience of it, we would not record what happened *exactly* the same way. In other words, we would not tell the same story. I would choose to emphasize aspects of the event that I think are important and relevant to the people I'm writing to, and you would do the same. We are both telling the truth but would highlight different aspects of the same experience.

I then told him to read the Gospels as though he were there in person—a spectator—as the events of Christ's life, death, and resurrection unfolded. What would it have been like to be in the presence of God? How would you react if Jesus healed you of an infirmity or disease? What does Jesus's life mean for you today?

He took the Bible and started leafing through it. I pointed out where the Gospels started and asked if he would like to pray together. He said yes, and I prayed for the repose of his dad's soul. I also said a prayer that the Holy Spirit would open his mind and heart to seek and to follow the Way, the Truth, and the Life. I prayed he would have the courage to follow the truth wherever it leads so that he can become the person that God created and is calling him to be. I thanked the Lord that he put us together, and I gave the young man a blessing. He thanked me and walked over to his girlfriend, who was watching us with great enthusiasm from another area. I pray that the young man will find what his heart is yearning for—the truth that will set him free.

The Truth Will Set You Free

My own faith (Sonja) was inherited, cerebral, and sadly minimal until my relationship with Jesus was ignited, and that only began when I became serious about obedience to daily prayer in the Scriptures. Unlike Deacon Harold, who is a "cradle Catholic," I grew up a Southern Baptist. As non-Catholics, we had no sacraments. The only way to get into direct contact with God was Bible reading and study.

So I embarked on a somewhat tentative, daily discipline of yawning (often sleeping!) through my thirty-minute sunrise Bible reading and was rattled to the core one day when God himself met me there. The spiritual sages had assured me he would if I would prove myself serious by persevering in the habit, but it was still something of a precious terror when part of the text seemed to come alive and leap off the page like an ember and burn its way into my heart. A cursory reading of "You will know the truth and the truth will make you free" became *I am the truth, Sonja Corbitt, and you shall be set free!*

Imagine my surprise when later, as a proud new Catholic, I learned (as a matter of fact) that our Baptist daily quiet time in the Bible was

3

not a clever Protestant invention, but one the Church has prescribed, taught, and practiced for millennia!

EVER ANCIENT, EVER NEW

Church history calls it *lectio divina*, Latin for "divine reading." Exactly when and how the actual designation came about is lost in the mists of time, but it was one that indicated a particular way of reading the Scriptures that was different from study or regular liturgical readings, one through which an individual lets go of his own agenda in reading and opens himself to what God wants to say to him.

Before literacy was common and the printing press was invented (around AD 1500), Bibles were hand copied by monks, exorbitantly expensive, and rare. People did not possess individual copies, and only a few would have been able to read them if they had. Lectio divina began sometime in early Benedictine monastic tradition, when the monks gathered in daily chapel to listen as a member of the community read from a communal copy of the Bible. Through this exercise, the monks were taught to consider what they heard to be direct communication from God, and therefore to listen to it with their hearts as the Word of God.

In the twelfth century, a Carthusian monk named Guigo formally described and recorded the stages traditionally considered essential to practicing lectio divina. Today, his stages remain fundamental and the monastic practice and discipleship in Scripture reading, meditation, and prayer that constitute traditional lectio practice continues to promote communion with God and increase the knowledge of his Word. As the Church has known and taught for centuries, the Bible will come alive for us when we begin approaching it as God's word to us, as direct communication to us about our individual lives.

> For in the sacred books, the Father who is in heaven meets His children with great love and speaks with them; and the force and power in the word of God is so great that it stands as the

support and energy of the Church, the strength of faith for her sons, the food of the soul, the pure and everlasting source of spiritual life.[1]

Indeed, God is always speaking to us through the Scriptures.

For this reason, the Church has always venerated the Scriptures as she venerates the Lord's Body. She never ceases to present to the faithful the bread of life, taken from the one table of God's Word and Christ's Body.

In Sacred Scripture, the Church constantly finds her nourishment and her strength, for she welcomes it not as a human word, 'but as what it really is, the word of God'. In the sacred books, the Father who is in heaven comes lovingly to meet his children, and talks with them (*Catechism of the Catholic Church* [*CCC*], 102–104).

In all of my life, I (Sonja) have found nothing so consistently transformative and fecund as the regular encounter with Almighty God in my daily lectio divina practice. He knows me more deeply than I know myself. His all-seeing eye penetrates with absolute freshness and clarity through the layers of my schedule, my circumstances, my past, my soul, my pretense, and my psyche. Perhaps you are sufficiently curious to begin trying it, so let's look at the mechanics of the lectio practice.

THE PROCESS: LECTIO, OR LISTENING

Traditionally, the first stage is *lectio* (reading), where we read the Word of God slowly and reflectively so that it sinks into us. Before you start, select your passage. Any text of Scripture can be used for this way of prayer, but the passage should not be too long, usually only ten or fifteen verses at most.

As Deacon Harold pointed out to his young friend at the conference, when one is beginning his journey in Scripture, it is easier and more fruitful to choose a passage from one of the Gospels. Because it connects us in the Word of God to the whole universal Church on any and every given day, we specifically suggest the Gospel reading for the Mass of the day as offered by the Catholic Church. Those are available in a print resource, such as the *Magnificat, Our Daily Bread,* or *The Word Among Us,* and online at USCCB.org or Universalis.org. I (Sonja) like the Laudate app for my phone and the Jesuit website Sacredspace.ie. Deacon Harold also uses Laudate, as well as iBreviary on a daily basis.

First, go to a quiet place, recall that you are about to read the Word of God, and—this is important—ask the Holy Spirit to speak to you. Then read the Scripture passage slowly, with full attention. Maybe you want to read aloud to let yourself hear the words with your own ears. Perhaps you'd like to emphasize each word, like this:

> *You* will know the truth, and the truth will make you free (John 8:32).
> You *will* know the truth, and the truth will make you free (John 8:32).
> You will *know* the truth, and the truth will make you free (John 8:32).
> You will know *the* truth, and the truth will make you free (John 8:32).
> You will know the *truth,* and the truth will make you free (John 8:32).

If you try this tip, continue emphasizing each word in the passage until you have stressed them all. You can see how slowly and meditatively lectio divina is meant to be practiced.

MEDITATIO, OR OBSERVING
The second stage is *meditatio* (meditation or reflection), where we think about the text we have chosen and ruminate upon it so that we

receive from it what God wants to give us. When you finish reading, pause and recall if some word or phrase stood out, or something touched your heart or piqued your curiosity. If so, pause and savor the insight, question, feeling, or understanding. Then go back and read the passage again, because it will have a fuller meaning. Pause again and note what happened.

Notice that what you are receiving is not strictly audible, but more of a mental apprehension, an understanding or thought that seems to somehow come from both inside and outside of you.

I (Deacon Harold) start my weekly Eucharistic Adoration time by meditating and reflecting on the opening verses of Psalm 63: "O God, you are my God, for you I long; for you my soul is thirsting. My body pines for you like a dry, weary land without water. So I gaze on you in the sanctuary to see your strength and your glory. For your love is better than life."

I (Sonja) like to journal the meditatio part, and I actually begin lectio after having journaled my current thoughts, fears, questions, and worries as a written prayer to God. Somehow the process of writing it all down helps me purge, focus, and recollect myself; apply the reading to my life; track progress; and gives me black-and-white evidence of God's movement and direction. But journaling is not a traditional part of lectio divina; it's not necessary, and you don't have to do it at all.

We do what works in hearing and obeying God. If journaling doesn't work for you, pitch it. But if it does, jump in! Ultimately, the reflective listening that is meditatio allows the Holy Spirit to deepen our awareness of God's initiative in speaking with us.

ORATIO, OR VERBALIZING

The third stage is *oratio* (response), where we speak to God about what we've read and meditated on. If you want to dialogue with God the Father or Jesus in response to the Word, you should simply follow the prompting of your heart without questioning the subtlety of what is occurring or the order in which you think you're supposed to do it. Like the cultivation of any other good habit, practice makes perfect. You may have to mentally refer to each stage in the lectio divina (simply lectio for short) process in the beginning, but it quickly becomes familiar and comfortable. I (Sonja) would say lectio is even absolutely necessary to my sanity.

During oratio, you might be so enamored or convicted by what you are hearing from God that you find yourself imagining you are hugging him, or face-planted at his feet in worship or repentance, or both. Any response is correct, even negative emotions. He's a big God; he can handle your ugly. In fact, because it is a relationship we are cultivating, intimacy with God is not possible without absolute honesty in prayer. The Bible itself is clear on that.

Whatever God says to us through the reading, and however we respond, we must take what we receive in the Word of God into our daily lives and allow it to change us. Otherwise, we deceive ourselves into believing we are following him simply because we have performed the act of reading the Bible.

> Be doers of the word, and not hearers only, deceiving your-
> selves. For if anyone is a hearer of the word and not a doer,
> he is like a man who observes his natural face in a mirror; for
> he observes himself and goes away and at once forgets what
> he was like. But he who looks into the perfect law, the law of
> liberty, and perseveres, being no hearer that forgets but a doer
> that acts, he shall be blessed in his doing. (James 1:22–25)

For me, then, the oratio stage usually involves some purpose of amendment, an action plan if you will: the addition or elimination of some specific behavior or action that I will begin implementing immediately, that very day, such as confessing and avoiding some sin

God has just brought to my attention through the reading; making a gift or sacrifice, restitution, or apology; erecting a boundary; taking specific action to change some habit or typical way of responding to others, and so on.

CONTEMPLATIO, OR ENTRUSTING

Once I have decided on some action with his help and in his presence, I am often overwhelmed by the tenderness, patience, mercy, forgiveness, and generosity of God. This is the final stage of lectio divina, *contemplatio* (contemplation, or rest), where we leave our reading, thinking, talking, and planning aside and simply let our hearts trust God. This is where we listen to the voice of God and allow that voice to change our lives.

The desire to be still and thankful in his peace and love is naturally inspired by and proceeds from all that has occurred to this point in our encounter with him in his Word. We should resist speech now, remain silent, and simply rest in him. In his presence we receive grace upon grace at the deepest level of our being and are gradually transformed from within. Obviously, this transformation will have a profound effect on the way we actually live, and the way we live is the test of the authenticity of our prayer (see James 1:22–25).

THE ONE THING NECESSARY

The primary focus in lectio divina is allowing God to speak to one's heart through the text, rather than necessarily extracting information from the study of it. One approaches the Bible as the living Word that it is: "For the word of God is living and active, sharper than any two-edged sword, piercing to the division of soul and spirit, of joints and marrow, and discerning the thoughts and intentions of the heart" (Hebrews 4:12).

Such an approach does not treat Scripture as texts to be analyzed, but as the living Word. Lectio is undertaken not with the intention of gaining information but of using the texts as an aide to contact the living God. Basic to this practice is a union with God in faith which, in turn, is sustained by further reading.

The four stages of lectio divina are not fixed rules of procedure, then, but simply guidelines in how the prayer normally develops. Its natural movement is towards greater simplicity, with less and less talking and more listening. Gradually the words of Scripture begin to dissolve, and the Word is revealed before the eyes of your heart.

But there is an important place for Scripture study. Scripture as a subject or discipline for a Christian is neither lectio divina nor study, but both lectio and study, heart *and* head. We'll talk about and help ease you into deeper study in later chapters.

But the wisdom of centuries of saints says to begin with lectio, meditation of the mind coupled with assent of the spirit, moving all the while from reflection to worship and back again. This animation of the Scriptures feeds the natural desire for information without overwhelming it. The fruits gained from lingering over a single word or phrase for an indefinite period of time is well worth the effort, knowing with full confidence that it will lead to further appreciation of the text at hand. Combine that with the Church's liturgical cycle, and you have, literally, a never-ending source of inspiration.

A Community Endeavor

When you read and study Scripture, you are not alone. You are part of an ancient and global community (Acts 2:42–47). It's more than an individual expression, because it also happens in and with the universal Church. Reading and studying Scripture is both an individual expression of love and trust for God, as well as a communal expression of our faith.

Lectio divina, then, can also be an effective form of group prayer, as those first Benedictine monks knew well. After a passage is read, extended silence is offered for each person to savor what he or she has heard, particularly noting whether any word or phrase became a special focus of attention. The group might invite members, if they desire, to share aloud (but without discussion) the word or phrase that struck them. Then a different person from the group would read the passage again with a pause for silence. Different emphases might be suggested after each reading: What gift does this passage lead me to ask from the Lord? What does this passage call me to do? The prayer can be concluded with an Our Father.

Whether one prays individually or in a group, lectio divina is a flexible and easy way to pray. One first listens, notes what is given, and responds in the way he is directed by the Holy Spirit.

If lectio is used for group prayer, obviously more structure is needed than for individual use. In group prayer, much will depend on the type of group. Lectio may involve discussing implications of the Word of God for daily life, but it cannot be reduced to this. The movement of the prayer is always towards silence. If the group is comfortable with silence, more time should be spent resting in the Word. "Be still and know that I am God" (Psalm 46:10).

Lectio divina as a way of praying the Scriptures has been a fruitful source of growing in relationship with Christ for many centuries, and in our own day is being rediscovered by many individuals and groups. In fact, Pope Benedict XVI said renewal will come to the Church in the new evangelization through a rediscovery of the Scriptures.

Diving deep into Scripture is the only way to truly ignite our understanding of who God is and what he wants for us and from us. "The Church has always venerated the Scriptures as she venerates the Lord's Body. She never ceases to present to the faithful the bread of life, taken from *the one table of God's Word and Christ's Body*" (*CCC*, 103, emphasis added).

Part of the "one table" of the Lord's provision for proper spiritual health, is to be fed by the Word of God. To be undernourished in the Scriptures is to be malnourished in faith as St. Jerome said: "Ignorance of Scriptures is ignorance of Christ."[2]

Let's Review

This is how to hear God speak to us through his Word.

- *God is calling me* to a deeper relationship to him through his Word.
- *The sacraments of the Church are only one half* of what constitutes proper spiritual nourishment.
- *The bread of life comes from the one table* of the Scriptures and the Eucharist (*CCC*, 103–104).
- *God is always speaking* to me through his Word.
- *Lectio divina, or divine reading, is the key* to an intimate, personal, on-fire relationship with Jesus Christ.
- Traditionally, *the four stages of lectio divina* are reading, meditation, prayer, and rest.
- *If I will commit to the daily discipline* of lectio divina, God promises to speak to me there.

Invitation

As Deacon Harold pointed out at the beginning of this chapter, trying to read the Bible from the beginning can be baffling. I clearly remember my utter frustration the first time I attempted to do so. I began in Genesis like anyone begins a book, but was quickly confused by the story of Adam and Eve's first sin. Genesis 3:7 says, "Then the eyes of both of them were opened, and they knew they were naked…" I wondered, *What happened in that moment of sin that made them know they were naked. What exactly?*

I finally skipped it but quickly ran into another wall: the book of Leviticus. Oh dear! Rule after rule after oppressive rule. Leviticus is such a dry, angry-seeming book. If I were a less tenacious learner, I would have simply gotten angry, assumed the Bible was stupid, and never picked it up again.

We do not want that to happen to you. We want the Scriptures to come alive for you; we want them to speak to you; to have hands that take hold of you; to have feet that run after you. So let's begin as the saints suggest: in the Gospels, with lectio divina, and let's do it together. Following the traditional steps of lection let's LOVE the Word.

L—Listen
O—Observe
V—Verbalize
E—Entrust

GOD PROMPT

Lectio—Listen

> Jesus entered Jericho and was passing through. And there was a man named Zacchaeus; he was a chief tax collector, and rich. And he sought to see who Jesus was, but could not, on account of the crowd, because he was small of stature. So he ran on ahead and climbed up into a sycamore tree to see him, for he was to pass that way. And when Jesus came to the place, he looked up and said to him, "Zacchaeus, make haste and come down; for I must stay at your house today." So he made haste and came down, and received him joyfully. And when they saw it they all murmured, "He has gone in to be the guest of a man who is a sinner." And Zacchaeus stood and said to the Lord, "Behold, Lord, the half of my goods I give to the poor; and if I have defrauded any one of anything, I restore it fourfold." And Jesus said to him, "Today salvation has come to this house, since he also is a son of Abraham. For the Son of man came to seek and to save the lost." (Luke 19:1–10)[3]

Oratio—Observe

Jericho, an enormous city rich on trade to the East, is surrounded by date palms and scented with almond flowers. Cumin, cassia, myrrh, and essential oils feed a continuous caravan of exports streaming away from the city like ant trails. For the Roman government, the city is an engorged center of taxation. Plump. Ripe. Spilling over with revenue. Neck-deep in the harvest are the tax collectors, making sure what is Caesar's is rendered unto Caesar, and in the process, a denarius or ten rendered unto their pockets.

It's early spring, and Jesus is passing through Jericho. If he is not stopped, he will keep going. Where will he pass me by today if I do not stop him?

The crowd swells as the curious vie for position. But for one man, curiosity isn't enough. He is Zacchaeus, a small man.

Zacchaeus must have learned early how to survive in a big world, as one who probably got pushed around and bullied and teased for his size. Maybe he learned to compensate, to laugh at the jokes, to stay invisible, and to bide his time until he was standing tall at the top where payback is hell.

In the difficult process of growing up, maybe a tender part of his childhood was trampled underfoot and crushed, squashed under the clumsy and often cruel feet of the big and tall. As he climbed the professional ladder, he must have carried that crushed bit of himself everywhere he went. Don't you?

Did he also step on anyone who stood in his way, anyone on the next rung up, until he arrived at the top, where people finally fear him? Not just tax collector, *chief* tax collector. That the Scriptures say he is rich is redundant. The modern equivalent is something like the drug boss with the gold grille, both in his mouth and on his car, filthy and rich on all that ruins lives. Zacchaeus has power; he has wealth. But he's despised and corrupt and alone, and now he's up a tree looking for Jesus.

What he sees up there, draped over the limb like drying laundry, is the total lack of a great Messiah-king's pomp or ceremony, and yet, something about Jesus is clearly royal. Every eye follows him as he parts the sea of spectators on his way to that sycamore, and a long-awaited sun shines on a despised bill collector. The one whose professional mantra has long been "Show me the money!" must now account for himself: money bribed...money blackmailed...money offshore...money skimmed off the top...money, money, money, money: the bottom line of a bankrupt life.

But Jesus isn't auditor. He is Savior.

Jesus is searching for the one who is searching for him. He sees Zacchaeus, into his heart, peering into the crushed soul under the swagger, and inside he sees every heel mark and footprint. And then Jesus presents himself as one in need: tired, thirsty, hungry.

We have to remind ourselves constantly of how genuinely human Jesus was, "like us in all things but sin." Where will Jesus present himself to me, today, as one in need?

Jesus asks for help from a person he was supposed to avoid and hate. He asks Zacchaeus for a place to stay.

Ripples of contempt for the two work their way through the crowd, but whispered innuendoes can't diminish the wealth of the moment. And, in the same way you would welcome a friend you have yearned to see for far too long, Zacchaeus goes out on another limb and welcomes Jesus home.

Look closely. Witness the miracle: it's a camel passing through the eye of a needle.

Meditatio—Verbalize

Dear Jesus, forgive me for trying to compensate for my stunted growth. I have expected my work and wealth to increase me. Today, help me to practice decreasing by serving those in need around me. Help me to recognize you in the opportunity, so I can truly increase in stature.

Like Zacchaeus, I long to see you. With my own eyes, I want to see you myself, see you for who you really are. Not through the eyes of a pastor or teacher or evangelist.

I've heard so much about you. How much is opinion? How much is hearsay? How much is truth? I want to know for myself. I want to hear with my own ears. Please come near, Lord, as you pass by today. I am out on a limb, waiting for you, out of my comfort zone. And as you come, overwhelm me with the wonder that it is not I who seek you in the streets, nearly so much as it is you who seeks me hiding in the trees.[4]

Contemplatio—Entrust
Perhaps you'd like to spend a few silent moments simply resting in his presence.

chapter two

The Who of the Bible

Not long ago, I (Sonja) was watching a Discovery Channel special on the physiology of death. In it was an interview with a woman who recounted a near-death experience, one of the most baffling to science, in fact, because she was clinically brain dead at the time of the alleged experience. She was able to accurately recreate the operating room setup, repeat conversations she heard during the surgery, and describe the surgical tools explicitly, all details that would have been impossible for her to have physically seen or heard because all brain function had been completely arrested due to the delicacy of her brain operation.

She talked about being drawn toward a radiant, perfectly serene light that emanated a love so powerful and absolute she never wanted to be away from it, and was aware that she had never experienced anything like it at any time in her life. She related that she recognized and was met by her grandmother, who prevented the woman from proceeding further down the dark tunnel toward the light. Because it was utterly brilliant and strange and irresistible, the woman reportedly asked her grandmother if the light was God. Her grandmother replied, "No, honey. That's what happens when God breathes."

THE HOLY OTHER

The story's veracity notwithstanding, it is true that God dwells in unapproachable light, whom no man has ever seen or can see (1 Timothy 6:16). Why is that? God is not a material thing, but pure

Spirit (John 4:24); there is nothing to see or measure or approach or discern of God at all unless he somehow makes himself heard, seen, felt, or sensed.

Additionally problematic in attempting to learn anything about God is that the human brain lives in a physical body that requires bits of time and sensory data to receive knowledge and information. How, then, does limited humanity get to know the "who" of the Bible, he who created and transcends both time and matter, someone whom physical senses cannot grasp?

One must allow him to speak for himself and trust that self-disclosure. This trust-in-self-disclosure is what we call faith. What God tells us about himself requires faith, because while the human intellect naturally seeks the essence of things under their form, it is restricted to knowledge of what is created; nothing we have seen or understood as a human race can resemble, fully express, or in any way apprehend him who is uncreated. God's "wholly otherness" is why "faith is the substance of things hoped for and evidence of things not seen" (Hebrews 11:1, NKJV). It's why as Christians "we look not to the things that are seen but to the things that are unseen; for the things that are seen are transient, but the things that are unseen are eternal" (2 Corinthians 4:18).

Person to Person

Surely, then, the most interesting, transformative thing about practicing lectio divina and receiving the Word of God through it is the precious terror of experiencing and building a relationship with the uncreated Holy Other who created me.

There, in the Bible, in his own words, we see that he is a living, personal God who insists on treating the persons he has made as persons too, by revealing himself to them. In encountering God in the Scriptures, we can then consider that the whole Bible is about this same gradual, increasing self-disclosure to a particular race of people just like me: the revelation of a person to persons, like ourselves, who also actually lived in a certain place at a certain time. Here's what we mean.

One of the most often presented examples of ancient biblical characters God has presented to me (Sonja) in my life with him has been Abraham (formerly known as Abram). Very early on, God used his exchanges with Abram to speak to me. In Genesis 15:1 the Lord presents Abram with a promise, "I am…your exceedingly great reward." Then Abram asks God something like, "Oh yeah? What are you gonna give me, then?"

I found that irresistible, because when I originally read that Abram was getting a reward, my own mind streaked wildly with thoughts of things I might desire myself. And my next thoughts were exactly Abram's response. *What will I get, Lord?* Oddly enough, just like Abram, God shocked me by promising me the very thing I wanted more than anything in the world. But God reveals the curious, primary prize to Abram. The Lord declares himself the reward.

I felt deflated. Did Abram? Do you? Can you think of something else you would rather have than God? Was Abram's reward worth the stress and difficulty it required to abandon his home, possessions, and family, and journey without knowing where he was headed or what awaited him there? Is it worth it to you? Can he satisfy your perception of the greatest reward you could ever receive?

Exceedingly means "vehemently, urgently." *Great* is from the root meaning "increase, heap up, multiply, abundant, blessed." He is your exceedingly multiplying, vehemently heaped up, exponentially increasing reward. What will that mean for you? Don't you want to know? Why do we read about Abraham without dying to *be* Abraham, to receive something from God beyond anything we could ask or think? He claims he is an exceedingly great reward. *Your* exceedingly great reward. Will you trust his self-disclosure?

We can say, then, that the Bible is simultaneously personal declaration and invitation. The truths revealed there did not descend from heaven by parachute, nor were they mined from prehistoric rock or beamed in from outer space. God has made himself known—not as an impersonal force or idea or set of rules, but as a relational person—in and through the living, relational experiences of human beings, culminating in the person of his own Son, the Word made flesh (*CCC*, 53).

Without flesh and personhood, the ancient words on the onion pages of the Bible are just words, words for other people in another time, perhaps, but not for me. But through their flesh and personhood, I can learn about God personally, his purposes and ways, his loves, and how he speaks to and interacts with me.

Certainly, God could have supplied us with a systematic list of dos and don'ts for belief and behavior, but it would have been too abstract and time sensitive to be useful. If such a directory had been expressed in the vernacular of a single age or generation, it would have been largely meaningless to all others. Instead, God revealed himself in personal situations, which, being human, are real, concrete, and readily intelligible in every generation. Their record in the Scriptures enables us to see for ourselves.

God's dealings with the people of the Bible are recounted for us between its pages, we are told, to "teach us" (Romans 15:4; 1 Corinthians 10:11). The faults, sins, failures, and brutalities of even the most heroic men and women of the biblical narrative are wholly retained so that we easily identify ourselves in them; they are "like us" (James 5:17; Acts 14:15).

There are candid warnings in their miseries. We get to see what happened when Noah got drunk; when Abraham fell so deeply into fear that he exposed his wife to mortal danger to save his own skin; when Jacob cheated; when Joseph bragged; when Moses threw a temper tantrum; when David became a thief, a murderer, and adulterer in a single act of sexual passion; when Peter denied, betrayed, and abandoned Jesus. Their unbelief, compromise, boastfulness, indiscipline, and disobedience are all fully displayed.

Yet they are truly great, precisely because they ultimately overcome the common temptations and doubts and fears natural to every soul. We witness their refusal to bow down to tyrannical, idolatrous governments and embrace martyrdom rather than renounce this God they have come to know and love so deeply and intimately: their belief in his promises in the face of every possible evidence to the contrary; their loyalty in an age of prevailing apostasy; their tireless service to their generations; their brave proclamations of truth in times when the masses have willingly become unmoored and are adrift in false narratives.

God encountered and transformed the biblical characters in the context of their settings of time and place, because he also wants to encounter and transform us in the context of our own settings of time and place. To understand him—his purposes and ways—we must understand his purposes and ways with them. God and men, both persons, are the "who" of the Bible.

First to a couple, then to a family, a tribe, a nation, a kingdom, and then to the whole world, God reveals himself to each of us limited persons in the only way we can receive him. Through his Word, he speaks just as he did then, "precept upon precept, precept upon precept, line upon line, line upon line, here a little, there a little" (Isaiah 28:10).

AN EVER-INCREASING SELF-DISCLOSURE

Before the sin separated their wills (and everything else) from him, the first individuals, man and woman, "walked" with him in the Garden in the "cool of the day" (Genesis 3:8). Noah and his family also walked with God in such intimacy (Genesis 6:9) that the human race was preserved in them.

Abraham, meaning "father of many," was the first to be named a "Hebrew" (Genesis 14:13), and as such he and his whole tribe "passed through" or "crossed over" from their homeland to an unknown place in order to obey and follow God. His pilgrimage in obedience would ultimately transform Abraham into such a perfect likeness of God the Father that he was willing to sacrifice his only son. Through his obedience, God was able to make him the father of the Hebrew race, "elder brothers" to us and all people of faith in Christ (*CCC*, 63).

After the patriarchs, God revealed himself even more fully to a whole nation, one he personally called and rescued out of Egyptian slavery through Moses for no other reason than that he "loved [their] fathers, therefore he chose their descendants after them" (Deuteronomy 4:37). To their leader, Moses, God offered some of the most exquisite mysteries ever revealed to the human race.

To Be, or Not to Be, That Is the Question

Moses stands on holy ground; he hides his face, afraid to look on the God calling him from the bush to deliver his people from slavery in Egypt through miraculous leadership and power (Exodus 3:1–6). In the face of the extraordinary presence and voice from inside the flaming but intact bush, somehow Moses has the presence of mind to ask God his name. Was he was trying to pin him down, possibly harkening back to the polytheism of Egypt, looking to identify him with some familiar god?

Whatever it was, anticipating their skepticism, "Moses said to God, 'If I come to the sons of Israel and say to them, "The God of your fathers has sent me to you," and they ask me, "What is his name?" what shall I say to them?' God said to Moses, 'I AM WHO I AM.' And he said, 'Say this to the people of Israel, "I AM has sent me to you"'" (Exodus 3:13–14).

The people of Israel had previously distinguished God only as the friend of Abraham, Isaac, and Jacob. Now they and the whole human race know his name.

A name expresses a person's essence and identity and the meaning of this person's life. God has a name; he is not an anonymous force. To disclose one's name is to make oneself known to others; in a way, it is to hand oneself over by becoming accessible, capable of being known more intimately and addressed personally. (*CCC*, 203)

The Whom Who's in a Name

Part of God's promise of deliverance is the assurance he would "be with" his people (Exodus 3:12), and he goes on to establish his presence with them in the tabernacle. Now he tells Moses his name is "I AM" (Exodus 3:14). This self-designation of God is from the verb *to be* and originates from the root *to breathe*. It means, "I exist, I breathe, I live, I am being itself, I AM." God is not only his own essence but also his own existence. Self-existent, uncaused, independent, self-identified, and self-sufficient, God was indiscernible to humankind until he self-disclosed and made himself known.

Did you know *to be* is the most prolific verb in every language? To be—was, is, will be; I am, you are, he is, she is, it is; we are, you all are, they are—isn't it a stunning polyglot realization that all that exists, all that was, is, and will be, proceeds from HE IS? Everything that *is* was created through the power in the Hebrew words that called it to be.

Unlike human speech—which once spoken is gone—God's speech is everlasting (Psalm 119:89) because he is everlasting. So his word remains active and operative, constantly re-creating and energizing the world.

Since everything was created through the words of I AM, the Hebrew name given an object was meant to express the very power that gave it existence. Rather than a simple moniker or title, names in the Scriptures are important. Ancient names were supposed to bear significance, so people's names expressed particular characteristics they possessed: Moses, meaning "drawn out," as in drawn out of the Nile River and later Egypt with God's people; Jacob, meaning "cheater"; and Emmanuel, meaning "God with us." Names were carefully and solemnly selected, especially personal names, because they explained, in part, who a person and what a thing *was*.

Researching biblical names often supplies information that would otherwise be missed by a simple reading of the text, so we look up almost every biblical name in a concordance.[1] So intimate was the relationship between individuals and their names that "to be called" something meant "to be" that something. Knowing one's name meant knowing the person behind the name. Likewise, to withhold one's name was to withhold the particular intimacy of the "is-ness" of a person.

This is why, in the Sacrament of Baptism, the very first statement is, "What name do you give this child?" God wants to know the name he will call that child forever.

By revealing his name, God declared and invited. Stooping down to peer into his friend Moses's face, he personally and tenderly offered himself in profound simplicity to all humanity as an invitation to an all-consuming intimacy: I AM WHO AM. Conveying the scope of this telling is like trying to cram the whole universe into an acorn cap. By saying next to nothing, the name says everything that is, and so exquisitely, as though he had nothing better in all of eternity to do than disclose to us his secret.

Who IS? He IS. And although *to be* is the most common verb in every language, he's the only one who truly IS. A traditional Jewish understanding of holiness helps explain what we mean.

Holy Terror

Typically, when we think of holiness, we think cleanliness or purity. The word holy literally means "other, set apart, sanctified, and consecrated." In the Old Testament, things and people were set apart exclusively for God, for the worship of God or for God himself to work, speak, and rule through. To preserve this unique otherness, sacred things and people were not to be used or even touched in ordinary ways.

Ancient Jews used triple repetition to express the superlative of holiness. For instance, we say holy, holier, holiest; they said, "Holy, holy, holy is the Lord God Almighty" (Revelation 4:8).

To the Jewish mind, this "otherness and holiness" means more along the lines of transparency. God is holy because he is who he is and nothing else. He says of himself, "For I the Lord do not change" (Malachi 3:6). Elsewhere, it says in him "there is no variation or shadow due to change" (James 1:17).

How will it feel to be in the presence of the one who is, and have every moment, every word, every action, every thought and motive of my heart from every second of my life be known and shown to me, absolutely, utterly, vulnerably, nakedly, to its root and foundation and core? We will know the second we die and return to the one who made us, and at that moment, our eternity will be sealed and irrevocable, because the limiting factor—the flesh—will have been removed. In the Bible, glimpsing oneself in the otherness of God's absolute transparency is felt as fear.

> On the morning of the third day there was thunder and lightning, and a thick cloud upon the mountain, and a very loud trumpet blast, so that *all the people who were in the camp trembled*. Then Moses brought the people out of the camp to meet God; and they took their stand at the foot of the mountain. (Exodus 19:16–18, emphasis ours)

Why was it terrifying and dangerous for the people at Mount Sinai when God appeared to them in the theophany and revealed his Law?

Because in God's absolute clarity, he sees who we are, and in him who is utterly transparent, we see ourselves as we really are too.

The more different from God we are, the more terrifying he is to us. The less similar our wills and our love, the more fake we are and the more terrible the experience of his seeing through us is. He insists, "You shall be holy, for I am holy" (1 Peter 1:16).

A relationship with him who is, by absolute necessity, must be founded on transparency. I must be who I am in I AM's presence, or I cannot know him for who he is, and we cannot be one. This holy transparency is why the Jews called I AM WHO I AM the excellent name, the great name, the only name, the glorious and terrible name, the hidden and mysterious name, the name of the substance, the proper name, and most frequently the explicit or the separated name.[2]

God calls us to complete transparency by revealing us to ourselves in his Word. As he reveals himself to us in his Word, we see ourselves more clearly. The more obedient to that Word we are, the more holy we become, until we—like Moses—are so transparent that he is operating through us without impediment.

Over and over, God revealed more and more of himself to Moses, thereby revealing more and more of Moses to himself, until after forty years in the desert of purification, he was transformed into the likeness of God so completely he was capable of leading God's whole people to freedom as a worthy forerunner of the Christ who would rescue us all from the slavery of sin. Moses became holy, effacing fully into the "is-ness" of his true dignity and calling as the Great Prophet, in the consuming fires of God's transparent love.

This people, led first by Moses and then the judges, the kings, the prophets, and finally Christ, "are Israelites, and to them belong the sonship, the glory, the covenants, the giving of the law, the worship, and the promises; to them belong the patriarchs, and of their race, according to the flesh, Christ who is God who is over all be blessed forever" (Romans 9:4–5). If the primary "who" of the Bible is God, the secondary "who" has to be the Israelites. It is the relationship between these two, and all of us by extension, to which the whole Bible testifies.

Let's Review

This is how God reveals himself as a person through people.

- *God describes himself to the human race as a "who"* not as a "what." God clearly identifies himself as a person, not an energy or force.
- *"I AM WHO AM" is God's name*—YHWH—in Hebrew, a revelation considered to be foundational for both the old and new covenants.
- *God's revelation of himself to Israel was an invitation* to a relationship with him.
- *The Bible is the story of God's gradual self-disclosure* to his people, to me, over time.
- *Jesus is the full and final, personal revelation of God.*
- *I learn who God is and who I am* by watching how God personally speaks to and interacts with the people of the Bible.

Invitation

When I read and study the Bible, I am reading and studying about real people like me. They were formed by their historical, national, and religious circumstances; so am I. Their lives revealed God's particular purposes; so does mine. How do they relate to me? What can I learn from them about how God speaks to and interacts with me, and from their understanding of God? In reading and studying the Bible we explore the Jewish people as the people of salvation and our spiritual ancestors, because we can understand something of the purposes and ways of God by knowing the people to whom God spoke and revealed himself.

What he says and does is the subject of our next exploration, the "what" of the Bible.

GOD PROMPT—*LOVE the Word*

Lectio—Listen

And the Philistine said to David, "Am I a dog, that you come to me with sticks?" And the Philistine cursed David by his gods.

The Philistine said to David, "Come to me, and I will give your flesh to the birds of the air and to the beasts of the field."

Then David said to the Philistine,

You come to me with a sword and with a spear and with a javelin; but I come to you in the name of the Lord of hosts, the God of the armies of Israel, whom you have defied. This day the Lord will deliver you into my hand, and I will strike you down, and cut off your head; and I will give the dead bodies of the host of the Philistines this day to the birds of the air and to the wild beasts of the earth; that all the earth may know that there is a God in Israel, and that all this assembly may know that the Lord saves not with sword and spear; for the battle is the Lord's and he will give you into our hand.

When the Philistine arose and came and drew near to meet David, David ran quickly toward the battle line to meet the Philistine. And David put his hand in his bag and took out a stone, and slung it, and struck the Philistine on his forehead; the stone sank into his forehead, and he fell on his face to the ground. So David prevailed over the Philistine with a sling and with a stone, and struck the Philistine, and killed him; there was no sword in the hand of David. (1 Samuel 17:43–50)

Oratio—Observe

David hears that the Philistine warrior Goliath the Goth has issued a challenge to the soldiers of Israel. Goliath has mocked and defied the Israelite army for forty consecutive days, but Saul's men are too afraid to confront such a formidable opponent.

It is easy to see why. Goliath was a truly intimidating figure, standing approximately nine feet, nine inches in height. He wore seventy-eight pounds of armor and had a spear that weighed just over nine pounds. In the presence of Goliath, the Israelites "were dismayed and greatly afraid" (1 Samuel 17:11).

Meditate on Goliath as representing today's secular culture, a culture that threatens and intimidates us with violations of religious liberty; that calls contraception "health care"; that commits egregious sins against children, the elderly, and a civilization of love and life; that attempts to force people of good conscience to violate the natural law by redefining marriage and penalizing everyone who does not accept this personal lifestyle-choice decision.

Many of us are so intimidated by the size, scope, and depth of this onslaught that we tremble with fear; we say and do nothing.

Maybe your battle against Goliath is more personal. What is the Goliath in your life that is preventing you from being the person God has called you to be? Is it pornography? Alcohol? Drugs? Contraception? Fear and anxiety? Depression? What is it that has you so scared that you are more comfortable living as a slave to sin rather than living free as a son or daughter of God?

The Goliaths in our lives cause us to fear and empty us of God's love. The flow of grace through daily prayer and the sacraments fills us with love so that we can truly be perfect ("whole" and "complete") in the eyes of God. "There is no fear in love, but perfect love casts out fear. For fear has to do with punishment, and he who fears is not perfected in love. We love, because he first loved us" (1 John 4:18–19).

Filled with confidence in God's love, we can then face Goliath with confidence:

The Lord is my light and my help;
whom shall I fear?
The Lord is the stronghold of my life;
before whom shall I shrink?
When evildoers draw near to devour my flesh,
it is they, my enemies and foes, who stumble and fall.
Though an army encamp against me
my heart would not fear.
Though war break out against me
even then would I trust. (Psalm 27:1–3)

Often our first attempts to face our Goliaths are feeble and ineffective because we move in our own power. "Saul clothed David with his armor; he put a helmet of bronze on his head, and clothed him with a coat of mail. And David belted on his sword over his armor, and he tried in vain to go, for he was not used to them. Then David said to Saul, 'I cannot go with these; for I am not used to them.' And David put them off" (I Samuel 17:38–39). At first, David tried to put on armor so he could look fearsome like Goliath, but he was unsuccessful. He realized that, for this battle, he needed to don the armor of God and fight with the weapons of faith.

It is useless for us to fight this culture war using only the conventional weapons of logic, reason, sound apologetics, and impassioned debate. There must also be a profound and overarching spiritual dimension that comes into play. By forming our minds and hearts in accord with the tenets of the Catholic faith, we put our faith into action daily, by living the Beatitudes, forming our consciences in accord with natural law, and loving God and our neighbor. "You see that a man is justified by works and not by faith alone…. For as the body apart from the spirit is dead, so faith apart from works is dead" (James 2:24, 26).

David "took his staff in his hand, and chose five smooth stones from the brook, and put them in his shepherd's bag or wallet; his sling was in his hand, and he drew near to the Philistine" (I Samuel 17:40). Looking at the literal sense of the passage, David had five stones in the event that Goliath's brothers sought retaliation against him over Goliath's death (cf. 2 Samuel 21:19–22; 1 Chronicles 20:5–8).

In the spiritual sense, the sling and stones are a type of rosary, each stone representing the Our Father bead and reflecting one of the mysteries of our salvation. They also represent the five wounds of Christ, our Lord's battle scars in his victory over sin and death. In our battle against the Goliath of the culture and within ourselves, the rosary is most certainly the weapon of choice. Satan cannot stand to hear the names "Jesus" and "Mary," which are repeated throughout the rosary.

David confronts Goliath. Unwavering in his faith and armed with a simple weapon, David embarks on what his kinsmen would surely have considered a suicide mission. They believed that David had no chance of defeating such a colossal enemy. After Goliath mocks David and threatens his life, David prevails upon God and with God when no one else dared.

There will be people in your life, possibly members of your own family, who will try to discourage and deter you from taking your faith to the next level. You may have even convinced yourself that the vices and addictions that control and enslave you are too powerful. When we think like that, Satan wins. Be prepared to excise from your life anything and anyone that causes, tempts, or leads you to sin, including friends, family, television, alcohol, and the Internet. Whatever or whoever it is that is leading you to hell must leave your life—now. Our decisions and actions in this life have eternal consequences.

Meditatio—Verbalize
Lord, I sense you are saying this to me through your word:

By the witness of my life and as an image of Christ crucified, in small ways, today, please help me send a clear and strong message to my culture that there is a God who saves, and his name is Jesus Christ. Help me remember that I am not alone in this fight—that the battle belongs to you, and you have already won the war through your victory over death on the cross.

Thank you for helping me defeat my own Goliaths, not through armor that is too burdensome for me to carry or weapons too oppressive for me to wield, but through the matchless power of the wounds of Christ and the small but mighty stones of the prayers and verses in my daily rosary.

Contemplatio—Entrust
Perhaps you'd like to imagine resting beside him in love and thanksgiving.

chapter three
The What of the Bible

I (Deacon Harold) remember when the birth of our first child, Claire, transformed a marriage, my marriage to my wife Colleen, into a family of three. It was also the first time I experienced the power of God's love in a deeply personal and meaningful way.

About eleven days before Claire was due, we were coming out of Mass, and my wife said, "I feel kind of funny." I took over, saying, "Don't worry, I'll take care of everything." When we got home, I helped her to the couch, put her feet up, and got her some lunch. A few hours later my wife said, "These pains are getting closer together. I think it's time for us to go in." Since the due date was still almost two weeks away, I told my wife that she might be experiencing Braxton-Hicks contractions, in other words, false labor. To make her feel better, we grabbed her delivery bag and went to the hospital. Colleen went into the examination room while I stood in the hallway with the bag thinking that we would be going home. A nurse came out and said, "Congratulations, you're going to be a dad…tonight!"

At 2:01 AM our daughter was born. It was an incredibly moving experience, but I knew that something was wrong. Instead of crying, Claire was gasping for air. The doctor, looking very concerned, cut the umbilical cord and called for the respiratory therapists. The doctor immediately handed our daughter to them and turned her attention back to my wife.

After my wife delivered the placenta, she began bleeding. As Colleen continued to bleed, the doctor walked across the room to a telephone and scheduled emergency surgery. Meanwhile, I saw them take our daughter to the NICU. I was now standing in the corner of the room watching everything unfold. I thought to myself, *It wasn't supposed to be like this. My wife might die and my baby might die, and there's nothing I can do about it.* I felt totally and completely helpless in the hours we were separated from our daughter as they tried to get her stabilized.

Finally, after hours of my wife saying, "I have to hold our baby," she was able to do so. Still lying weakly in bed, we had to push my wife's hospital bed right up against the incubator because the breathing tube wasn't very long. The nurse picked up our daughter and placed her in my wife's arms, and that was the first time Colleen got to hold our child. My wife held Claire tenderly and began to caress and talk to her. I stood back and watched this beautiful scene unfold while my mind raced through the history of our relationship: from dating to our engagement to the wedding day…and now she was holding our baby.

After a few minutes, my wife turned to me and said, "Your turn." It was then I realized that I never got a chance to hold Claire myself. As I gathered my daughter into my arms, I experienced an incredible outpouring of love as I had never experienced in my life. It was as if every ounce of love in my body was spilling into this precious, beautiful baby. I thought to myself, *My God, I actually helped to make another person. My wife and I did our part, God did his part, and here she is.* I said to Claire, "Hello I'm your father." And then I thought, *How am I going to pay for college?*

The thought that struck me most, however, was, *This is what God's love must be like.* The intensity of the love that I experienced in those first moments holding my daughter was like a drop in the ocean compared to the depth of the love that God has for each of us, as if we were the only person that has ever been created. I knew without a doubt that God's love was real.

I also understood that the God of love calls every one of us into a relationship of intimate, personal, loving, and life-giving communion. He is inviting us to share his life and the life of his whole family! Our response to God's invitation to intimacy and communion is to be the person he created and calls us to be—to make a gift of ourselves—because, as my daughter taught me on her birthday, when we give ourselves away in love, we truly find ourselves.

No matter who it is or what time period of history, every family begins with a man and woman and eventually grows into bigger families, tribes, nations, and kingdoms, siblings and grandparents and cousins and uncles and squabbles and feuds and glories. God's family history is like every family history: messy. At its most basic, the Bible's "what" is simply the story of God's family, its "Once upon a time", its failures and feuds, and its wars and glories. It is how God worked and spoke through all of it and why, and how it all shakes down in the end.

Isn't one of the first issues anyone confronts when beginning to read, study, and love the Bible some confusion regarding what it's about? Understanding the Bible's purpose explains to us why and how we should read it, because a person's approach and expectations have a lot to do with what he or she gets out of Scripture.

THE BIBLE IS A BOOK OF SALVATION

The sacred Scriptures are "his-story," a sort of five-act play, if you will: the creation and fall; the story of Israel, the race of Jesus; the story of Jesus; the story of the Church; and the foretelling glimpses of a new creation.

Knowing, understanding, and adjusting our lives to "his-story" can save us from sin; it offers abundant life, wholeness, and peace. The Bible's "what," then, is first of all salvation. Because God "desires all men to be saved and to come to the knowledge of the truth" (1 Timothy 2:4), we read the Bible in order to know all that pertains to salvation. And what we discover is that God, from the first moment of creation, has always had a plan to save us.

Perhaps we think of salvation as a never-ending heavenly timeline moving off into an eternal future of worship. When I was small, I (Sonja) told my mother I didn't want to go to heaven because all we'd be doing there is singing forever, and ever, and ever...

What if, instead, salvation has everything to do with my life and daily circumstances right now? What if salvation means much more than a place called heaven? What if salvation is a quality of life, God's own life? The Bible teaches that God invites us to share in his very own quality of life. What do you imagine the quality of God's life to be like? Is his existence satisfying? Full of purpose? Overflowing with goodness and happiness?

God accomplished his self-revelation as Savior in unfolding historical situations, through a nation called Israel and a person called Jesus Christ. So it can never be divorced from its historical context or understood apart from it. Christianity, then, is a historical religion.

But the Bible is not a history book in the sense that it offers a full and objective account of the facts of a certain period. Instead, the Biblical chronicle flows from personal testimony of the prophets of God's family that God had "done this for no other nation" (Psalm 147:20). Their selection of material shows their writing to be the confession of faith of a people rather than a detailed record. The historians of Israel showed concern for the past and present fortunes of other nations only as they affected those of Israel and Judah, two tiny territories on the edge of the Arabian desert which few had ever heard of.

For instance, ancient Sumer, Egypt, Babylonia, Persia, Greece, and Rome—all mighty empires and rich civilizations—are only alluded to or included in the narrative as context for the dramas of Israel. The fascinating prehistoric animals, such as dinosaurs; the famous architecture, such as the Sphinx and Pyramids; the great thinkers, such as Aristotle and Socrates; the military heroes, such as Hannibal and the gladiators are never even mentioned.

Instead, the scriptural record concentrates on men and women who saw God face-to-face and lived, who actually, literally spoke with him, and lived and died for him, men and women whose footsteps still seem warm from treading deserts and palaces in obedience to him. The focus of the Bible is not on the wisdom and wealth and learning of the world—all of that is recorded elsewhere. The "what" of the Bible is God's salvation of man and the relationship between the two.

The sweep of this sacred history is magnificent, telling the whole family story of man from God's point of view, from Creation to the New Creation, from the beginning of time to its end (Genesis 1:1; Revelation 21:1, 5). Christians divide history into BC and AD, indicating the periods before and after Christ as the axis of all human history. In the same way, the Bible is divided into two halves, the Old Testament looking forward to and preparing for eternal salvation in Jesus's arrival, and the New Testament telling the personal stories of his life, death, resurrection, and ascension, and the implications of it all until the end of the world.

CREATION

Beginning with creation, the Bible's story is given to us in a library of seventy-three books (forty-six in the Old Testament and twenty-seven in the New Testament) arranged by literary genre, rather than chronology. The first five books are called the Pentateuch, meaning "five scrolls" or "five tools." They do tell a mostly continuous story and are therefore (except for Leviticus) relatively easy to read.

Our simple, unadorned creation narrative is superficially similar to ancient and prolific Near-Eastern myths in that both begin with chaos and end with some kind of organized cosmos. But Genesis differs from those coarse, polytheistic, immoral, and even grotesque accounts in its personal wisdom, dignity, ethic, and sublimity.

The Bible begins by elevating primordial cosmology to the majesty of God's forethought and careful planning. The Lord of creation, God of the whole universe, is not a national mascot like the gods claimed by other nations. He is personal, and personally involved in all the making and processes. The Genesis account is deliberately told from humanity's perspective on earth, but it is God-centered in the sense that the whole initiative of creation lies with him: God did it, all of it, out of nothing, however it was done (Genesis 1; *CCC*, 338).

Like great secular literary epics, the genre and language is stylistic and not necessarily meant to be understood literally. The world may have been created in seven twenty-four-hour days or a few thousand or billions of years ago; the stars and planets and our various biological life forms could have been created instantaneously or evolved over time; maybe man's body developed from previous biological forms, maybe it didn't; regardless, it all must be ultimately attributed to God and his plan, for Scripture records: "All things were made through him, and without him was not anything made that was made" (John 1:3).

Furthermore, the Catholic faith insists on the unequivocal historicity and uniqueness of man: that the human race descended from a real, original pair and sin from their actual fault (*CCC*, 390), and that the "human soul is immediately created by God"[1] so that the individual soul does not evolve and is not inherited.

If I were to pick up a Bible and try to read the creation account in Genesis apart from the historical teaching of the Church and/or without its primary purpose of salvation in mind, I might conclude that the Bible teaches scientific error. Do you see why it is important to know the inherent truth that the Bible teaches regards salvation, rather than science?

The Bible is not necessarily interested in scientific accuracy because science is based on physical observation. The Bible's concern is what is spiritual and therefore unobservable; spiritual truth must be revealed.

There are inconsistencies, inaccuracies, and discrepancies in what the Scriptures are *not* trying to teach (areas that have nothing to do with salvation). For example, Genesis 1:1–2:1 says seven days were required for God to create the visible world. Do you believe this is meant literally or figuratively? Light was created on the first day (Genesis 1:3), but the sun was created on the fourth day (Genesis 1:16–19). How do we explain this?

After Cain killed Abel, God placed a mark on him "lest any who came upon him should kill him" (Genesis 4:15). Where did these other people come from?

Scientific theory suggests evolutionary processes of millions of years, but however long it took, the biblical text presents itself as a literary epic, not a science text. Creation events are framed in three symbolic pairs in which the fourth and first "days," the fifth and second "days," and the third and sixth "days" correspond. Within this literary structure, God gives form to what is "formless" and fills what is "void and empty" with all the diversity of life and matter we have evidence of, know, and experience.

And then he turns the whole stunning, pristine, cosmic work of art over to the stewardship of the newly made, plain human creatures as a shocking gift that they seem to take for granted and fail to appreciate. Suffering and death enter and spread through and with the human experience.

BC Civilization

The Genesis account of Adam and his descendants in chapters three and four seems to imply a Neolithic civilization in which monogamous marriage, cultivation, husbandry, and "city building" (probably a rudimentary village) all took place. A few generations later we read of those who played the "lyre and pipe" and forged "instruments of bronze and iron." We witness the rapid increase in wickedness of man and society after the Fall, resulting in the punishing Flood that seems to have spread throughout the Fertile Crescent, the known world at that time. The repopulation of the Earth begins with Noah and quickly spreads. Civilizations are established. Architectural structures are built. The tower of Babel appears to resemble a Babylonian ziggurat (a rectangular tower with steps).

A series of narrowing genealogical tables focuses our attention sometime after 2000 BC, when God calls Abraham, the first to be known as *Hebrew* (Genesis 14:13; "one from Eber," meaning "to cross over" or "to pass through"). Patriarchal history begins with Abraham's journey out of Ur in Mesopotamia to a new country with specific promises: "I will establish my covenant…between me and you…to be your God and the God of your descendants after you" (Genesis 17:7).

Later known as the essence of God's covenant, the promise is repeated over and over again throughout the Old Testament. *Testament* means "covenant." Rather than a legal document that is temporary, a biblical covenant is, as Dr. Scott Hahn teaches, a permanent exchange of persons: God gives himself to his people, and the people give themselves to God.

Abraham's covenant was renewed with his son Isaac, and Isaac's son Jacob, whom God later renamed Israel, so that Jacob's sons were the original "children of Israel."

That family of twelve squabbling sons went on to father whole tribes, the twelve tribes of Israel, who lived, not yet in the land promised to Abraham, but as slaves under the Egyptian pharaohs of the Great Pyramids. As the innumerable people of God labored under their Egyptian masters, they cried out for deliverance. "God heard their groaning and he remembered his covenant with Abraham, with Isaac, and with Jacob" (Exodus 2:24), and he sent them a Hebrew kinsman who had grown up in Pharaoh's palace, specially prepared by God to deliver them.

THEIR FAITH STORY, OUR FAITH STORY

The whole Old Testament can be—and is, repeatedly, throughout the Bible—summed up in the sweeping story of the Exodus. In an account that remains, to this day, a picture of our own Christian life, God rescued his people from slavery, led them through barren desert scarcity to deeper knowledge of him, and onward to the richness of the Promised Land flowing with milk and honey.

He made them a nation under a great prophet, gave them a unique rule of law summed up in the Ten Commandments, a renewed covenant relationship, and a system of liturgical (ceremonial) worship, all of which unified them under their God. As one family, they observed a liturgical system of holidays and rituals that both memorialized and preserved their national identity while preparing them for a Savior who would deliver the whole world and draw it into God's embrace as one great family.

The books of Exodus, Numbers, Deuteronomy, and Joshua recount the Israelites' escape from Egypt and partial conquest of Palestine, while Leviticus is their liturgical worship manual. Judges through Esther and the Maccabees detail the system of judges that led to their kings and kingdoms; characterize their rule, reign, tragic split, and captivities; and give us some history through the great empires up to the advent of Christ. Job through Sirach contain the wisdom literature of the people, a sort of moral science or philosophy that contains their collection of beautiful cultural songs, prayers, poetry, parables, and proverbs.

As the people multiplied and conquered the surrounding nations of the Promised Land to make it their own, they also adopted foreign political and religious ways. The children of Israel enthroned kings, for instance, and fell into the idolatrous religious practices of the people around them.

So God sent rounds of prophets to speak in his name and warn them to cleave to him and all he had personally and uniquely revealed to them or face the inherent consequences of giving themselves to things and nations that did not love them. Repeatedly he warned that those nations and things would turn on them and use them unmercifully. The rest of the Old Testament is a series of those prophets' warnings, through which we also get glimpse of the coming Messiah they predicted.

AD CHRIST AND HIS CHURCH

When the fullness of time had come, when all the preparations had been made and history was ready, God sent his Son to show us, ultimately, what he is like. The Gospels tell the eyewitness story.

In repeated displays that scandalized those in the family who thought they knew him perfectly already, Jesus showed us God is humble. God is our Father. To save us from the more lasting slavery of sin and death, he willingly placed himself into murderous hands and sacrificed himself out of love. He was crucified. He died. He was resurrected and seen afterward. He ascended into heaven, the gospel writers witness.

The book of Acts tells us the story of the birthday of the Church, an assembly of even greater scope in which the non-Jewish were welcomed into God's family. The epistles, or letters, of the apostles and those close to them offer us the first written teachings that circulated ("encyclical") throughout the Church and formed the basis of the New Testament. Finally, the great holy book closes with mysterious symbols and prophecies common to apocalyptic literature of ancient times.

Getting a feel for the general "what" of the Bible, what it's about, is imperative when reading and studying it. We might liken the "what" to having a map of the forest that prevents our becoming lost or disoriented among the trees.

One example is that a cursory reading of the first five books (the Pentateuch) reveals that God ordered the total annihilation of entire cities, nations, people groups, and civilizations—men, women, children, property, and animals. People who read the Bible often question us about why God seems so brutal and exacting in the Old Testament. They have trouble reconciling the Old Testament God with a tender, child-blessing, forgiveness-teaching Jesus; they feel the Testaments seem to be at odds with one another.

AN ONION STORY

The Bible, and salvation history contained therein, however, is laid out a little like an onion—you peel it from the outside in. Old Testament scholars tell us God is probing and correcting the literal, visible, outward behavior of his infant people in the Old Testament. He is very strict, the punishments are quick and sure and even seem harsh at times. He leads them to the desert, kicks all their props out from under them, and teaches them to depend on him there for provision: literal food and water, physical protection from human enemies, civil laws, national rulers, and religious leadership. He gives them repeatable animal sacrifices and trains them in ceremonial worship because he wants them to draw close to him.

The Old Testament lessons are those of children. God's Old Testament people came from the polytheism of Egypt, had no idea what worshipping one God meant, and they did not have the indwelling power of the Holy Spirit to help them recognize or live up to the deeper standard of grace. They were spiritual children. With children, boundaries must be clear and tight and the consequences quick and obvious; this is to ensure their safety and to prepare them to think and work more deeply when their development is ready for it.

In the same way, the Church teaches that God provided outward behaviors and boundaries through the Law of Moses that would keep his Old Testament children safe and teach them to properly worship the one true God, until he could lead them to the advent of the New Testament Messiah. At that point he could move to deeper truths, inward behaviors, with a truly upward, heavenly momentum.

Because the family of God had been outwardly tutored, disciplined, and kept safe by the Old Testament law throughout their history, God could begin probing and correcting the spiritual, invisible, inward behavior of his more mature New Testament people at the proper time (see Galatians 3:23–25).

When history and the family of God had matured and developed enough to handle deeper truths, he was faithful to give himself completely to them in Christ, and the deeper, spiritual reality that he is. Jesus used those familiar Old Testament images to teach profound new spiritual truths. He spoke of the bread of *eternal* life, *living* water, *spiritual* enemies and territory, *heavenly* authority and leadership, *spiritual* worship and sacrificial offerings.

The principle is outward to inward. The Old Testament addressed the outside. *Outward* concerns behavior. When we read and study the Old Testament, we must keep in mind the purpose, the "what" of the Old Testament.

> God, the inspirer and author of both Testaments, wisely arranged that the New Testament be hidden in the Old and the Old be made manifest in the New. The books of the Old Testament with all their parts acquire and show forth their full meaning in the New Testament and in turn shed light on it and explain it."[2]

The New Testament includes and addresses the interior soul along with the outward behavior. *Inward* includes our interior perceptions and beliefs, the real motivations underneath our outward behaviors.

An Upward Spiral

Here's another way to look at it: One of the most fascinating subjects I (Sonja) explored in school was the winding double helix structure of DNA. If uncoiled, the DNA in all the cells in your body would stretch ten billion miles—from here to Pluto and back.[3] All this biological information, the code of life in each human body, is packaged in two corresponding, winding, ladder-like strands. God works a little like this also: in our outward behavior and inward motivations, simultaneously, in an upward-directed spiral leading straight into his arms.

The great Catholic spiritual directors and writers in history all describe the paradox of the Holy Spirit's simultaneously outward-to-inward and upward spiral action. Once again, the Old Testament children of Israel illustrate the same. When we study the two-hundred-mile journey of God's family from the slavery of Egypt to the land he promised and led them to, we discover this interesting (although possibly frustrating) principle in the most literal way. God's poor family's week-long journey turned into a forty-year marathon. They went around Mount Sinai over and over and over for forty years.

In the Scriptures, the number forty is derived from the number of gestational weeks in a pregnancy and symbolically represents periods of trial, testing, and waiting. The biblical use of the number forty has one underlying focus: it is a journey that always leads to a spiritual time of growth and change. Granted, forty years in scriptural terms simply means something like, "However long it took, it was the right amount of time." But the Scriptures convey that however long it was, it was long enough for a lazy, doubting generation to be replaced by one that dared to fight for the Promised Land.

Not just once, but throughout their history, God's children repeatedly found themselves under the control of one kingdom or another.

After Egypt, there was Assyria and Babylon, and later, Rome. God rescued them from their slavery to one nation; they were vigilant to obedience for a while, then got lazy and fell into bondage again to another. In their misery, they would cry out to God, who would rescue them from slavery. In all their wandering and all their falling and all their leaving God, they never ceased to be God's people, and he never abandoned them. He always provided for and loved and cared for them.

For us, too, the principle is the same as the onion and DNA metaphors: throughout our lives and circumstances, we travel around and around the mountain of God in an upward spiral to him. We are rescued from sin habits and fall into new ones. However, we are not covering the same ground over and over. Instead, we move upward toward him, learning things we need in very small, gentle upward degrees with every revolution.

Can you see then, how the Old and New Testaments together are not just a family history but also a metaphor and template for your own life with God? Just like our scriptural ancestors, the Holy Spirit began telling me (Sonja) the truth through the Scriptures about my outward behaviors and then moved steadily more interiorly. And he will do the same with you.

OUTWARD, THEN INWARD

I (Sonja) spent a lot of time and energy in my early twenties pursuing holiness and getting rid of the "big sins" in my life. Because I was in the church ministry, I felt I had to conquer these glaring faults, such as my smoking addiction and overdrinking. The obsessive perfectionist in me didn't want to be so obviously hypocritical. I started with smoking, which killed two birds with one stone since I always smoked when I drank. Next I quit cursing—a difficult prospect, since I had a filthy mouth, but I knew it was unladylike and ungodly. In all of these pursuits, which took considerable time, God led me step-by-step, sometimes second-by-second, and leaning completely on him, I was able to conquer these areas.

You can imagine my discouragement, then, when God began prompting me about my hidden faults. I began studying the effects of sin, including mistakes and things I felt I couldn't help. My raging temper? I can't help that, I would think, as I put holes in walls and deflated the spirits of other people with my rages.

By that time, however, God had gripped my soul, and I wanted nothing less than to please him. I was willing to hear that I had to follow Jesus down this narrow road in order to strive for the holiness that would bring me closer to God, and the prospect of being rid of an explosive pain I had carried my whole life became my Promised Land.

That I *could* help my rage and that I was responsible for changing it was the most daunting prospect, more so as God began to reveal how deeply the roots were buried.

Healing the Father Wound

I (Sonja) confess that anticipating Father's Day used to almost make me sick with anxiety. As much as I loved my dad, and still do, every year when June rolled around, I got an awful sinking feeling. I would spend hours in one card aisle after another, trying to find something that might somehow both honor my father, and still be truthful. "You are the best father in the world" was not a sentiment I felt comfortable offering my own dad.

If Father's Day makes you feel this way, you are not alone. So many people carry wounds from relationships with fathers, stepfathers, priests, grandfathers, and others that negatively affect their relationships with God and other men. It is an epidemic that fuels rebellion, homosexuality, promiscuity, rage, and all manner of sin in the Church and in individual Christians.

As Father's Day approaches, there is a Scripture that comes to my mind frequently: "For you did not receive the spirit of slavery to fall back into fear, but you have received the spirit of sonship that enables us to cry, 'Abba! Father!'" (Romans 8:15). The word *Abba* means "Daddy" in Aramaic. What a precious, intimate thought this verse is to me now.

But there was a time when it made absolutely no sense to me at all. Due to a lifetime of military and highway patrol, my dad was authoritative to the extreme, aggressive, controlling, and dominating. He seldom looked at me with love unless in a depressive, maudlin state, or my achievements made him look good to his peers. He rarely touched me with anything but anger, and almost never spent one-on-one time with me. I loved him almost as desperately as I was terrified of him.

As St. Paul warns us parents, I was provoked to wrath and discouragement by his parenting style (Ephesians 6:4; Colossians 3:21). I struggled with rage, rebellion against authority, and perfectionism for many years.

Yet, this strange verse beckoned me with its promise of a Father's gentleness and warmth. I once had an aunt who told me she imagined herself in God's lap when she prayed; she said she called him Daddy, and that one day I would too. I thought she was crazy.

But in Romans 8:15, St. Paul speaks of our cherished status as God's children, and he does so in several other places in the Scriptures, too. I discovered that John 1:18 speaks of Jesus as being in the bosom of the Father. Over and over in the Bible, Jesus applies the term Abba to the Heavenly Father. I wondered, what did Jesus know about God that enabled him to call God his Daddy and rest in his lap so affectionately? Together, all of these verses seemed to whisper to me that I was somehow a slave to my fear of God.

Although I longed to, how could I ever call God Abba? I obeyed him out of fear and a desire to make him love me. I thought every bad thing that happened to me was God's punishment, and that I must surely deserve it. I felt in the deepest recesses of my being that he was perpetually displeased with me. When he was quiet during my prayer, I assumed I had done something that deserved the silent treatment. If I was criticized by a man in authority over me—husband, employer, pastor—I struggled with volcanic eruptions of agonizing emotion. Because my relationship with my earthly father was so painful and difficult, I simply could not relate to God with such an intimate term as Abba.

If this is you, if you have a father or mother wound, if you are a parent who fears passing one on to your children, I want you to know that freedom was my Promised Land, and God led me there every painful revolution around the mountain, every fall into self-medication, toxic relationships, destructive circumstances, and overwhelming desire.[4]

I pray you too will seek God's healing in the Scriptures. Trust in the truth of these Bible stories and verses. Watch as Jesus shows us very deliberately, through the Scriptures in the sorrowful mysteries of the rosary, what it means to have a safe place to acknowledge weakness and receive strength in the midst of great pain and suffering. Listen carefully to his great prayer, the Our Father, as Jesus teaches us, his brothers and sisters, how to reach beyond our deficits to God, and how to climb into the lap of a loving heavenly Father.

The truth is our woundedness provokes grave sin patterns that we repeat throughout our lives until we can forgive those who sinned against us, so human and wounded themselves, and forgive ourselves for what we have done out of this pain. Our relationships suffer because we vomit this awful, festering poison all over everyone we love. But when God heals us, he heals them all too.

We fear we will never get victory over it, that we will never be in control of ourselves, that we can never forgive. But we can, and we must. It is our calling as God's children. Just like the children of Israel, it is also our freedom and our salvation. You only have to trust

God's promise, and obey him at every step, every single day. He is waiting for you with unconditionally open arms.

I am living proof that God longs to heal our wounds, and the word *salvation* actually means "healing, wholeness, integration, peace." The greatest joy and the deepest pain in my life have been the excavation of this father wound. I tell everyone who will listen how my Abba did it for me, a writhing, pitiful mess of a little girl searching for a daddy's love in places and people who could never touch her abyss of need.

THE BIBLE REVEALS THE GOSPEL

The time is now. This healing is the whole "what" of the Bible and its purpose, and as part of his family, you are entitled to the privilege. In speaking to humanity through the Word, God unveils his relational nature in order to invite us into intimate, personal, loving, saving communion and relationship. The greatest intimacy, insight, and knowledge we can have into the essence of God and his love for us shines forth in Jesus Christ, who accomplishes God's saving work.

Jesus is the final, complete, and absolute power and triumph of a relational God. His-story is in the Scriptures. The entire Bible witnesses to him (Revelation 19:10). Jesus said, "I am the way, the truth, and the life" (John 14:6). Jesus is the map, the Gospel (meaning "good news") message and the messenger, and the communicator of this salvation. He proclaims and transmits the kingdom realized and present in himself.

LET'S REVIEW

This is what the Bible is about.

- *The Bible's "what" is the story of God's human family and their salvation.* Their faith story is our faith story.
- *The Bible is a book of salvation.* Everything pertaining to the salvation of humanity is contained within, and nothing necessary to salvation was left out. The Bible is not primarily a book of

science, history, philosophy, or literature, and cannot be understood if read as such.

- *The principal purpose of the old covenant was to prepare for the coming of Christ.* The books of the Old Testament, according to the state of humanity before salvation through Christ, reveal the knowledge of God and of humans, and the ways in which God deals with humans. These books, though they also contain some things which are incomplete and temporary, show us true divine teaching.
- *The Old Testament primarily addressed the outward behavior* of God's people in order to prepare them for the inward behavior and deeper motivations and perceptions addressed by Jesus in the New Testament and his Church.

INVITATION

The Old Testament story is both the root and skeleton of the Christian story. We, too, were called individually by God to God, and rescued from the control and slavery of sin through Jesus, our sacrificial Lamb and Messiah-King. He leads us into the barren desert-valley of tears, teaching us through the scarcity. He nourishes us through the daily manna of the Eucharist and the Scriptures. We grow to potential in the sacramental life and community of the Church family under our Heavenly Father.

We wander away in sin, giving ourselves again and again to things and constructions that cannot and do not love us, only to learn how deeply he does when he welcomes us back into his bosom in tender forgiveness. Season by season, faith to faith, year by year, he teaches us to know and love him, trusting him completely for every provision in preparation for the Promised Land of eternal bliss with God.

What was the most significant sentence, idea, or paragraph you read in this chapter? If you are amenable to making marks in your books, we invite you to mark sentences or sections that stand out for you in some way. We often draw light bulbs or jot notes next to important sentences or ideas in books we are reading. If anything particularly struck you in this chapter, could it be the voice of God acting and moving in your heart and life?

God Prompt—*LOVE the Word*

Lectio—Listen

And he said, "There was a man who had two sons; and the younger of them said to his father, 'Father, give me the share of property that falls to me.' And he divided his living between them. Not many days later, the younger son gathered all he had and took his journey into a far country, and there he squandered his property in loose living. And when he had spent everything, a great famine arose in that country, and he began to be in want. So he went and joined himself to one of the citizens of that country, who sent him into his fields to feed swine. And he would gladly have fed on the pods that the swine ate; and no one gave him anything. But when he came to himself he said, 'How many of my father's hired servants have bread enough and to spare, but I perish here with hunger! I will arise and go to my father, and I will say to him, "Father, I have sinned against heaven and before you; I am no longer worthy to be called your son; treat me as one of your hired servants.'

"And he arose and came to his father. But while he was yet at a distance, his father saw him and had compassion, and ran and embraced him and kissed him. And the son said to him, 'Father, I have sinned against heaven and before you; I am no longer worthy to be called your son.'

But the father said to his servants, 'Bring quickly the best robe, and put it on him; and put a ring on his hand, and shoes on his feet; and bring the fatted calf and kill it, and let us eat and make merry; for this my son was dead, and is alive again; he was lost, and is found.'" (Luke 15:11–24)

Oratio—Observe

Between my second and third years of graduate school, I (Deacon Harold) had an opportunity to study theology in Rome. All expenses were covered except for the airfare, which I couldn't afford. When I told my mother what I was planning to do, she gladly gave me the money.

However, a day or two before purchasing the plane ticket, I received a phone call from my mother. She informed me that my younger brother was in prison, was in serious danger of losing temporary custody of his son, and that I was to send the airfare money to bail my brother out of jail.

This news didn't sit well with me, and I was sorely disappointed. I reminded my mother that I was the one who was Mr. Responsible, which was the nickname given to me by my family as a teenager. I was the one who became an Eagle Scout. I was the one who left the monastery to run the house and take care of the family while she recovered from open-heart surgery. I was the first in the family to go to college (to the University of Notre Dame, no less!) and now had the opportunity of a lifetime to study theology in Rome. I was the one who spent most of my life putting others first and myself second.

I also reminded my mother that my brother dropped out of high school. That he quit the Navy. That he had three children from three different women and never really put forth the effort to be a real father to them. He was the one who, through his entire life, thought only of himself. I told her that this is an opportunity for my brother to realize the seriousness of life and that imprisonment may be the key to turning his life around. My mother listened patiently to my plea and, in the end, made the decision that any mother would:

she told me how proud she was of me, that she loved me, and then ordered me to send the money.

But what hurt me more than not going to Rome was that I didn't even get so much as a thank-you from my brother or any acknowledgment of the sacrifice that was made for him.

A few years ago, I attended my twentieth high school reunion in Newark, New Jersey. When my brother found out I was coming home, he absolutely insisted that I stay with him. He picked me up at the airport, and we drove back to his apartment. He had purchased a brand-new bed just for me. He had a hot breakfast ready and waiting for me every morning. He gave me unlimited use of his Lexus SUV. He had a very responsible and demanding job at which he excelled. He now took great and loving care of his children, making sure that they got to meet and spend time with their uncle. We stayed up until three in the morning most nights talking, playing guitars, and watching action-adventure and horror movies just as we did as kids.

I was deeply impressed with the change that had occurred in my brother's life. I was proud of him and asked him, "What made the difference?" He looked at me with a face that I'd never seen from him before, and he said, "I know how important that trip to Rome was for you, and I wanted to show you that the money didn't go to waste."

The prodigal son had come home, and this time, the older brother embraced him with the Father.

Meditatio—Verbalize

Lord, I acknowledge the absolute mess I have made here…

Over and over you have provided generously for me, and I have taken it for granted, wasting opportunity after opportunity. To make matters worse, I have resented it when you welcomed back into your embrace people I consider worse sinners than I.

I am sorry. I am in need, and I want to be found. I hear you calling me back to yourself. Please give me just a glimpse of you waiting for me on the horizon so I can make those final steps home to life in your embrace and family.

Contemplatio—Entrust

Maybe you'd like to rest in the promise of your homecoming in this passage.

chapter four

The Where of the Bible

In my (Sonja) early twenties, my husband and I traveled to Poland on a mission trip. We stayed with a family in their small flat for two weeks, and it was a favorite trip abroad because it was such an un-touristy experience. We stayed where the locals lived, dined on what the locals dined, and learned to behave like Poles. We ate dinner leftovers for breakfast and drank beverages with no ice. We walked almost everywhere, but if driving was necessary, we rode with our hair on fire in a propane propelled two-door speck through cobble-stoned streets with no speed limits. We bathed once a week in cold water and slept on pallets on the floor near warm, exquisitely painted coal stoves. I relished it!

A couple of days into the trip I developed a sinus issue due to the changes in climate. I couldn't figure out why the locals kept offering me grape-flavored calcium tablets I knew wouldn't give me relief, so I hit the village street in search of something with a like-ness to Sudafed. A couple of futile hours later, I realized nothing of the allergy relief sort existed in the tiny village we were visiting, and maybe not in the whole country. But that wasn't the only humbling realization I experienced.

Because I was ecstatic to be there, I greeted everyone I met in the lane with a huge smile and "halloo!" But not one person returned my smile or greeting. All eyes were downcast, every face was solemn, and each attitude was close to fearful. I was depressed myself by the time I returned to the flat.

Curiosity beat out my fear of offending, so I asked our host family about my experience in the village, and they spent two hours relating personal stories of recent horrors in Polish history at the hands of communists, including extermination and exile from their homeland. Suddenly, I understood my cheerful attitude was clearly out of place, and I was humbled by the resilience of the nation that had welcomed me into its bosom.

Many people read the Bible as simply some kind of spiritual book, as if it were detached from history, events, people, consequences, and sequences. But it is our sacred history. If the whole process of revelation has been a self-disclosure of a person to persons, if God entered history as a person through a particular race of people at a special place in the world during a specific historical time, and if that same Jewish race of people also experienced and wrote most of what's in the Bible in and from that particular geographical place, what might the "where" of the Bible tell us about God?

Just like he did in the times of the Scriptures, God wants to speak to us through our own time, work, relationships, and geographical location. But to understand his ways with us, we must understand his ways with them. For that, we must know something of the when and where and through whom it all happened. We must be able to visualize the places, because the people and time and land constitute the unique scene in which God chose to speak, act, and intervene.

Isn't it fascinating that almost every human author of every book of the Bible was a part of the area of Palestine? Every biblical prophet, with the exception of Moses, who was buried with his obstinate flock outside, lived at least a little while in the Holy Land. They all lived and wrote from that context; we cannot understand Jesus, or ourselves as people of faith, without that context.

"If the firstfruit [of Judaism] is holy, then the lump [of Christianity] is holy; and if the root is holy then so are the branches" (Romans

11:16). Because we Christians are "grafted in" to the olive tree of faith (Romans 11:17), to know something about the land it grows in is to know something about ourselves in Christ. What interesting stuff might topographical, agricultural, climate, and geographical information contribute to our understanding of the Bible and ourselves in Christ?

THE NAVEL OF THE EARTH

To this day, the Land of Israel is more than simply a place for Jews. Because they do not formally recognize Jesus as their Messiah, they do not believe the Old Testament prophecies have been fulfilled for them. The Jews continue to believe in the literal, physical fulfillment of those promises in the same ways that the events of the Torah were literal and physical.[1] The land then, to them, is of primary importance, said to be a body for the soul of a people.

A Jew does not travel to Israel, they say, but returns there. Israel is a land with a soul of its own, a divinely blessed land; it is a specific, well-defined, very special piece of Earth to which Jewish destiny is tied and that is central to their existence. Jewish tradition teaches:

> God created the world like an embryo. Just as the embryo begins at the navel and continues to grow from that point, so too the world. The Holy One, blessed be he, began the world from its navel. From there it was stretched hither and yon. Where is its navel? Jerusalem. And its (Jerusalem's) navel itself? The altar.[2]

Following our elder Jewish brothers in the faith, St. Jerome and Christian geographers in the Middle Ages also argued that Jerusalem was the center, or the "belly button," of the world.[3] A stone set in the floor of the ancient Church of the Holy Sepulcher, the traditional site of the burial and resurrection of Christ, marks what is thought to be the exact spot.

Oddly enough, Tiberius, one of the four Jewish Holy cities and the capital of Galilee, expands the "navel of the earth" idea to include the entire Holy Land. Situated in the northern center of the land of Israel, its name is closely related to the Hebrew word for navel, and Jewish tradition ascribes that messianic renewal will originate in the city of Tiberius. Jesus's first miracle at Cana, his calling of the twelve disciples, and most of his public ministry all took place around the lake of Tiberius, also called the Sea of Galilee.

Named for the Roman emperor and established in the early Roman period, Tiberius was built by Herod Antipas, son of the Herod that massacred the innocents. He was the Herod who beheaded John the Baptist and played a minor role in Jesus's execution. After the Jewish revolt and sacking of Jerusalem in AD 70, the center of the Jewish population moved to Galilee so that Tiberius became the religious, administrative, and cultural center of the Jewish nation for the five hundred years up to the Arab conquest. Tiberius was one of the four sacred cities in Israel and the last seat of the Sanhedrin, the Jewish supreme court of the ancient land of Israel and forerunner of our own Magisterium. Many of the most important post-Bible, Jewish books (Mishna, Talmud) were composed there, as it was the home of many Jewish scholars.

A PEOPLE OF THE LAND

Although not in a purely geographical sense, Christians might argue that Palestine is indeed the "center of the nations" (Ezekiel 5:5) because it is our Holy Land too. Take a moment and locate it on a map. Bibles often included such maps in the back, but any map of the Holy Land will do.

A region distinct from all others, it is the center of world history and geography in the sense that it is the Promised Land that God pledged to Abraham two thousand years before Christ was born, lived, and died there. In this holy land, Christianity was born, survived the Roman Empire, and changed the course of world history. Like anything else, God didn't choose the location because it was holy; the land is holy because God chose it as the location for revealing himself. For those who believe in providence, the Palestinian setting for the love story of salvation cannot be accidental.

The word *Palestine* originated from the root Philistine, the notorious Israelite enemies and people of Goliath. The Philistines are first mentioned in the Bible as descendants of Noah (Genesis 10:14), who occupied a small southwestern section of the area called Philistia. From a simple geographic point of view, the land of Palestine bridges the European, African, and Asian continents, all of which converge at the eastern seaboard of the Mediterranean, and their citizens have always mingled on the trade routes by sea and land. Consequently, Palestine has been invaded from all three directions, but its location ultimately became a distinct advantage when the beautiful Gospel feet began trekking in all directions to evangelize the world for Christ.

In its widest sense, the "holy land" includes the whole Fertile Crescent, that great sweeping semi-circle from Mesopotamia and the Euphrates, the area where God called Abraham, to Egypt and the Nile, where baby Moses was "drawn out" of the river reeds to become the prince. Look at a map and notice the shortness of the distance between Egypt, Mount Sinai, and the eastern side of the Jordan River. How long do you think that foot-journey to the Promised Land should have really taken?

Judaism's very first journey begins with the quest for a land, and the first divine revelation to the very first Hebrew (Genesis 12:7) makes the promise of that land central. In fact, much of four out of the five books of Moses (the Torah or Pentateuch) tells the unfinished story of a people on a tumultuous journey to their promised land. And the touching scene we are left with, as we close the last of the five books, features a broken Moses on a mountaintop, hungrily overlooking the land of his dreams. Sadly, only his yearning gaze would make its way across the border into the holy land. Moses dies with his generation on the eastern side of the Jordan, and Joshua goes on to lead the people into their promised land of "rest" (Psalm 95:11).

And yet we Christians are also meant to enter into the land of rest: "'Today, when you hear his voice, do not harden your hearts.' For if Joshua had given them rest, God would not speak later of another day. So then, there remains a Sabbath rest for the people of God; for whoever enters God's rest also ceases from his labors as God did from his" (Hebrews 4:7–10).

The Israelites had not entered God's rest by historically entering the Promised Land. David's psalm, written almost three hundred years after Joshua led the people into the land, had warned his generation not to harden their hearts so they could enter God's rest. Like David before him whom he quotes, the author of the book of Hebrews called his generation more than a millennium later, and now calls all of us who read it presently, to respond to God *today* through the Scriptures:

> Let us therefore strive to enter that rest, that no one fall by the same sort of disobedience. For the word of God is living and active, sharper than any two-edged sword, piercing to the division of soul and spirit, of joints and marrow, and discerning the thoughts and intentions of the heart. (Hebrews 4:11–12)

The Bible says as they were exiles, strangers, and pilgrims (Hebrews 11:13), we are exiles, strangers, and pilgrims (1 Peter 2:11), and altogether we will receive the final realization of the Promised Land that still awaits us in the kingdom of God as one family (Hebrews 11:39–40). The message of the Bible, then, is clear: We are a people with a land!

GEOGRAPHY OF A PEOPLE

In a narrower sense, the ancient land of Palestine is the Promised Land. A rich, fertile land naturally separated into four geographical strips running north to south, it was "a land flowing with milk and honey" (Exodus 3:8) and "the most glorious of all lands" (Ezekiel 20:6, 15). The land was so fruitful that the spies who were sent in to reconnoiter brought back a single cluster of grapes so heavy it had to be carried by two men (Numbers 13:23–24). Although Palestinian farmers work hard to produce such a yield, Moses's description is accurate to this day:

> For the Lord your God is bringing you into a good land, a land
> of brooks of water, of fountains and springs, flowing forth in
> valleys and hills, a land of wheat and barley, of vines and fig
> trees and pomegranates, a land of olive trees and honey, a land
> in which you will eat bread without scarcity, in which you will
> lack nothing, a land whose stones are iron, and out of whose
> hills you can dig copper. And you shall eat and be full, and you
> shall bless the Lord your God for the good land he has given
> you. (Deuteronomy 8:7–10)

If the fruitfulness of the actual land of Palestine was a metaphor for the spiritual fruitfulness of the Promised Land in Christ, what might that mean for me?

The country is relatively small, extending only about two hundred miles north to south and one hundred miles west to east at its widest point, and it is protected by natural boundaries. The Lebanon mountain range extends to the north (*Lebanon* meaning "white" for its snows), the Mediterranean Sea to the west, and unforgiving deserts to the east and south. Dan was its northernmost city and Beersheba the southernmost, so that a popular expression denoting the land from north to south was "from Dan to Beersheba" (Judges 20:1; 1

Samuel 3:20; 1 Kings 4:25). Does the total area in square miles of the land of salvation history surprise you?

Imagine the shape of a wide, cursive V. On either side of the Jordan river valley, the trough of the V, called the backbone of the land, the hills roll upwards to the central highlands and back down to the coastal plains and beaches of the west, and to the eastern tablelands and back down to the vast Arabian deserts of the east. The topography of the land naturally separates it into four long, vertical, striplike divisions: the lowland Coastal Plains, Central Highlands, Jordan Valley, and Eastern Highlands.

COASTAL PLAINS

From west to east, the Coastal Plains ascend from the Mediterranean, where the marshes and luxuriant pasturelands supported David's flocks, and swaths of wildflowers like the "rose of Sharon," and "lily of the valley" (Song 2:1) bloomed in profusion. The plains roll gently upward from the coastal seaports to the Central Highland mountain range. The mountains from the central and eastern highlands tower over the plains and can be clearly seen from the coast.

CENTRAL HIGHLANDS

Jesus's childhood and public ministry took place in the highlands and hills of Galilee, and on a clear day, the Mediterranean Sea is visible only seventeen miles to the west. At the foot of the Carmel mountain range rests the main mountain pass to the south that leads to the hill country of Judea and Jerusalem. The region between was the focus of Israel's history during the divided monarchy, as the capital of the northern kingdom of Israel was Samaria and the capital of the southern kingdom of Judah was Jerusalem.

Jerusalem itself is built on a mountain surrounded by mountains, sometimes called the seven hills of Jerusalem, perched on the crest of a central highland mountain chain which stretches through Palestine from north to south. "As the mountains surround Jerusalem, / the Lord surrounds his people" (Psalm 125:2). The temple is said to have been built, destroyed, and rebuilt on the temple mount in Jerusalem on the very site on Mount Moriah where Abraham almost sacrificed his son Isaac (Genesis 22:2; 2 Chronicles 3:1). Pilgrims passed that way by donkey, camel, and foot for thousands of years.

Across the Kidron Valley below Jerusalem, the Mount of Olives offers a panoramic view of the temple site. From here, Jesus wept over Jerusalem, and the Mount of Olives has been a Jewish cemetery from antiquity based on the Jewish tradition (Zechariah 14:4) that when the Messiah comes, the resurrection of the dead will begin there. And so it did: The Mount of Olives is where Jesus ascended into heaven (Acts 1:11–12). From the summit of the Mount of Olives, the land runs a two-day foot journey through barren land, called the Wilderness of Judea, where Jesus was tempted by the devil for forty days.

The Jordan Valley

The Jordan River (*Jordan* meaning "descender") rests in a fault line in the valley. The river serves as a natural spine between the two mountain ranges west to east, and two smaller bodies of water in the area, descending in elevation from the northern snow-capped peaks, carpets of wildflowers, and twinkling waters of the Galilean hill country and lake of Tiberius to the lowest point on Earth in the south at the Dead Sea.

Also called "the Arabah," meaning "dry," the summer climate at the Dead Sea is consistently around 110 degrees Fahrenheit. Extreme evaporation and lack of rainfall keep the concentration of mineral deposits too high to support life, and the water level remains constant despite fresh inflow and absence of outflow. It is thought that the stench, desolation, salt, and pitch fires that destroyed Sodom and Gomorrah were caused by a volcanic eruption and earthquake on the fault line in this area (Genesis 19:24–29).

John the Baptist lived in the honeycombs of caves near the Jordan River and baptized Jesus in its water. The first Jewish and Christian hermits lived in this area, and the Dead Sea Scrolls were found in water pots left forgotten for millennia in caves where only goats can climb.

The desert of Arabah continues southward from the Dead Sea to the Gulf of Aqaba where Israel's kings kept fleets of ships to trade with Africa and Asia by sea (1 Kings 9:26). The Gulf of Aqaba meets the Red Sea at the tip of the Sinai Peninsula and flows onward to the Indian Ocean, making copper exports from nearby mines and imports of "gold, silver, ivory, apes, and peacocks" (1 Kings 10:22) easy and accessible.

THE EASTERN TABLELAND

The Jordan Valley ascends on the eastern side of the river back up higher still to the eastern highlands where Jacob wrestled with, and finally received his blessing from, the angel at the Jabbok River. The eastern tableland is a fertile plateau due to considerable rainfall. Bashan is known for its prolific flocks. Gilead is famous for its balm of Gilead. And the caravan of Ishmaelites that bought young Joseph from his jealous brothers was traveling on the King's Highway trade route from Gilead to Egypt on camels loaded with spices, balms, and myrrh (Genesis 37:25). Further south lies Mount Nebo in Moab, a land famous for its flocks, where Moses glimpsed the Promised Land for the first time. At its southernmost point is Edom, where the children of Israel were blocked from entering the Promised Land through the territory, and its inhabitants became lifelong enemies thereafter.

PEOPLE OF THE FLOCK

Early on in their history, the land was such that the livelihood of God's people relied perhaps more than anything else on their enormous flocks. Sheep and goats supplied milk, meat, wool, and the black hair from which the Bedouin tents they lived in, and even the Old Testament tabernacle, were made.

The shepherd led his sheep with his rod and staff rather than driving them: he knew his sheep, he called them by name, and they knew his voice and followed him. The relationship between flock and shepherd developed so intimately that God revealed himself as the "Shepherd of Israel" who gathers the lambs in his arms and gently leads those who are with young (Psalm 80:1, Isaiah 40:11). Shepherding was a metaphor in the ancient world and agrarian society that people intimately understood. The land of Israel was full of sheep and shepherds.

Shepherds spoke of care and feeding and protection, as in perhaps one of the most tender passages in all of Scripture, Psalm 23:

> The Lord is my shepherd,
> I shall not want;
> he makes me lie down in green pastures.
> He leads me beside still waters;
> he restores my soul.
> He leads me in paths of righteousness
> for his name's sake.
> Even though I walk through the valley
> of the shadow of death,
> I fear no evil;
> for thou art with me;
> thy rod and thy staff,
> they comfort me.

Jewish tradition says it was Moses's tender way with animals that endeared him to God as the great prototypical Jewish leader.[4] Tending sheep was the mainstay of our Israelite ancestry. Abraham,

Isaac, Jacob, Rachel, King David—all biblical greats—herded goats and sheep.

It was a man's job, and a lowly, humble one. Unskilled and high risk, shepherding was messy and dirty and solitary. Because shepherds lived apart from society and were largely nomadic, it was mainly the job of single males without children.

The shepherd knows his sheep and calls them by name, leading them to food and water and away from dangerous grazing areas. He doesn't just take the sheep to pasture and leave them there; the shepherd stays with his sheep through long hours, protecting them.

Sheep have no natural defense at all. At night, every shepherd brings his sheep into the village fold where they are all shut up together for the night. The wolf prowls about outside, the panther leaps over the enclosure, and thieves and robbers try to climb over the wall and fleece or even slaughter the sheep. But a massive wall of stone crowned with thorn bushes encircles them for protection from such predators and thieves. Once the sheep are inside for the night, the shepherd sleeps in the opening or door. The sheep cannot wander in the dangerous night without stepping over the shepherd. They sleep near him, enclosed with him, throughout the night.

In the morning, the shepherd with his crooked staff is the first to leave the little fortress. One by one, he counts his fleecy charges. He knows his sheep; he calls them by name. The sheep know their master's voice, and they follow him. The sheep will not follow a stranger. The shepherd is committed to protecting them at night in the fold, and in the morning leading them out by name, one by one, to green pastures and still waters. The shepherd is even the door; they pass by him to be identified as his own (cf. John 10).

The main duty of shepherds was to keep their flock intact and protect it from thieves and predators. Shepherding was dangerous, as wolves, mountain lions, and even bears often preyed on otherwise defenseless sheep. David fought off lion and a bear with bare hands, while tending his father's sheep, making him the model shepherd (1 Samuel 17).

Because shepherds were absolutely responsible for sheep, they were called to account for attacks and losses: "If the sheep be torn in pieces, then let him bring a piece for a witness" (Exodus 22:13).

Hired hands, or "hirelings" as one translation says, care nothing for the sheep. They're in it for the money, so to speak. They make no attempt to gather the owner's beloved sheep when they're scattered by wolves and other beasts (Zechariah 11:6). The Old Testament talks about the leaders of Israel in terms of hirelings who fleece and destroy the sheep and flee when danger comes. The sheep become victims of hirelings.

Jesus tells us to be cautious of hired men who are not shepherds and whose sheep are not their own, who, when they see a wolf coming, run away, leaving the sheep with the wolf that destroys them. We must be wary of the false shepherds of this age, who blind our eyes with rhetoric and close our hearts to truth. The Good Shepherd loved us so much that he laid down his life for us. In turn, we, the flock, must place all of our love and trust in our Lord and Savior Jesus Christ, and in him alone: "Know that the LORD, is God. / It is he that made us, and we are his; / we are his people, and the sheep of his pasture" (Psalm 100:3).

Sheepherding was so integral to the people's identity that when Israel's tribe was introduced to Pharaoh—the king of a nation which deified sheep and abhorred those who handled their god—they announced proudly that they were shepherds. To his question, "What is your occupation?" they replied, "Your servants are shepherds, both we and our forefathers" (Genesis 47:3). What is it about sheepherding that made it a favored pastime and the ultimate career choice of our saintly ancestors?

PILGRIMS' PROGRESS

Livestock farming is a nomadic vocation that involves mobile animals and caretakers rather than fixed and stationary land. Shepherds retain a sense of transience and impermanence that farmers do not, due to their commitment to the land they nurture. The farmer's fate is linked to a permanent patch of earth. That's where his energy and livelihood is invested.

Sheepherding for our forefathers and mothers, then, was not just a matter of practice but of principle, motivated by the fear of becoming tied to, and emotionally involved, with a land not their own.

Eventually, they did enter and settle the land, however, at least in part. And the stability settlements lent facilitated crop cultivation. The three major products of Palestine are often grouped together in biblical passages. "The Lord your God will bless the crops of your land—your grain, new wine, and oil" (Deuteronomy 7:12–13). The fruitfulness of their crops (or lack thereof) in the new land was a tangible mark of their trust in and obedience to God (Hosea 2:8; Joel 2:19; Psalm 104:15), so that agricultural labor was tied up with spiritual and moral attitudes.

Grain crops and bread were mostly wheat and barley. Wine production from extensive vineyards (also a metaphor for the people of God) was plentiful, as was the abundant oil from olive groves. Olive trees are particularly hardy in dry climates and shallow soil. Other fruits of ancient Israel were pomegranates and figs, so that the dream of prosperity for the ancients in the Messianic kingdom was, "Every man will sit under his own vine and under his own fig tree, and no one will make them afraid" (Micah 4:4).

Farming in ancient Israel was not an easy matter, as Palestine's location between the Mediterranean Sea and the desert produced unpredictable rainfall. For a good harvest the land was entirely dependent on rain. As with all agricultural endeavors, the Israelites knew no greater blessing from God than the early and latter rains (Joel 2:23–24).

The Palestinian rainy seasons are generally predictable, even if the rain itself is not. Summer extends from May/June to September/October, and during these five months, rain is scarce, so that Samuel's prayer for rain during wheat harvest was a request for a miracle. Indeed, "snow in summer and rain in harvest" are as misplaced as "honor for a fool," Proverbs says (26:1). During the dry season only dew and morning mist offer moisture, both so welcome that God uses them as a picture for his daily grace "I will be as the dew to Israel." (Hosea 14:5).

From about mid-October on follows the rainy season. These "early rains" were indispensable to cultivation (James 5:7). Summer heat and sun baked the earth to iron, so that without the early rains, plowing was impossible (Deuteronomy 28:23). But once the rains had started and begun to soften the soil, especially if their arrival was late, the farmer took advantage of the weather to plow and sow his fields in time for harvest, usually with oxen or donkeys. The early rains were followed by harrowing and weeding.

If the early rains of the rainy season from November were essential to plowing, the latter rains at the end March and April were essential to reaping. "Be glad, O sons of Zion, and rejoice in the Lord, your God; for he has given the early rain for your vindication, he has poured down for you abundant rain, the early and the latter rain, as before. The threshing floors shall be full of grain, the vats shall overflow with wine and oil" (Joel 2:23–24). Rain swells and matures the crops for harvest, which usually began with barley, around mid-April.

Harvest was an important time, and laborers were usually hired especially for the occasion. When the fields were ripe for harvest, the laborers put in their sickles (John 4:35), and the corn was tied into sheaves and shocked. Later the bundled and shocked corn was carried by camel or donkey to the threshing floor, a flat, hard, dirt surface at the top of a local hill. First it was threshed by animal hoof or sledge (Isaiah 41:15), then winnowed. Tossed into the air by pitchfork, the precious golden grain would fall to the earth to be collected while the wind blew the chaff away.

Harvesting grapes and winemaking were also happy harvest social occasions. Treading winepresses and separation of wheat from chaff became common images for divine refining and judgment (Luke 22:31; Revelation 19:15), and notice they are both times of celebration.

The in-gathering of the grain harvest, refreshing summer fruits that helped supplement the usual diet, and grapes lasted until August and September, while the last olives were picked in November.

The early and latter rains, sometimes called autumn and spring rains, were the necessary prelude to a good harvest. God linked the rain and harvest together as a promise of his care and protection: "And if you will obey my commandments which I command you this day, to love the Lord your God, and to serve him with all your heart and with all your soul, he will give the rain for your land in its season, the early rain and the later rain, that you may gather in your grain and your wine and your oil" (Deuteronomy 11:13–14).

Wise farmers knew to wait patiently for both the early and latter rains, and were full of thanksgiving to God for the crown of the year when the valleys are mantled with grain:

You care for the land and water it;
    you enrich it abundantly.
The streams of God are filled with water
    to provide the people with grain,
    for so you have ordained it.
You drench its furrows and level its ridges;
    you soften it with showers and bless its crops.

You crown the year with your bounty,
  and your carts overflow with abundance.
The grasslands of the wilderness overflow;
  the hills are clothed with gladness.
The meadows are covered with flocks
  and the valleys are mantled with grain;
  they shout for joy and sing.
(Psalm 65:9–13)

One reminder that thanksgiving and worship were due to the Lord for multiplying their crops and flocks came through Israel's festivals, part of the "when" of the Bible that we'll explore in the next chapter.

Looking toward Our Homeland

The land of the Bible roots the events of salvation history within a particular place chosen by God, the center of which was Jerusalem, and imprints the power of God's love within the physical and spiritual memories of God's people.

Spiritually speaking, the Holy Land is not just a patch of hilly earth or a dot on a map. The name of Jerusalem has an alternate meaning: "complete awe," denoting a whole way of life where one is so in touch with God as to be in constant worship and thanksgiving for all he has provided as we journey toward him. It's that secret place within each and every one of us where we are one with God and deeply in tune with his presence, so that Jesus could say, "the kingdom of God is within you."

When we are rooted in Christ, we are one with him and each other, the whole family of God from the beginning. Like the Jews before us who determined not to lose sight of the essential dream and promise of a homeland, we want to similarly always maintain a transitory sense of non-arrival. The children of Israel, unfortunately, all too often endured actual exile at the hands of hostile nations, but they were ever-conscious of always journeying. "For we are strangers before thee, and sojourners, as all our fathers were; our days on the earth are like a shadow, and there is no abiding" (1 Chronicles 29:15). "Our homeland is in heaven and it is from there that we are expecting a Savior, the Lord Jesus Christ" (Philippians 3:20).

LET'S REVIEW

This is the setting of the Bible's story.

- *The setting of the Bible is the land of Palestine,* the location from which the Gospel was sent out.
- *The Holy Land is important to understanding the Bible* because it is the setting from which God chose to reveal himself.
- *The Jews (Jesus and the apostles) are a people of the Holy Land;* Christians' final holy land of promise is the presence of God in heaven.
- *The Jordan River is the backbone* of the holy land.
- *The four geographical divisions of Palestine* are the Coastal Plains, Central Highlands, Jordan Valley, and Eastern Tableland.
- *Husbandry and agriculture are the two main occupations of the Bible,* and God likens himself to both the vinedresser and shepherd of his people.
- *Early and latter rains were absolutely necessary* to the people's survival, and they trusted God to provide for both.
- *We are a pilgrim people* on a journey to the Promised Land of heaven.

INVITATION

The township of Alexandra, situated about seven miles north of Johannesburg, is one of the poorest areas in all of South Africa. Its approximately 180,000 residents—an amount almost equal to the size of the entire city of Portland, Oregon—are squeezed into an area the size of Magnolia, Arkansas. The settlements along the Juskei

River, located well below the flood plain, have populations that exceed five hundred residents per acre. Alexandra also has a huge number of squatter camps made up of more than 34,000 shacks, which are one-room dwellings made of sheet metal, aluminum, and cardboard about thirty-five square feet in size, that house entire families.

The increasing number of residents, unplanned development, and overcrowding make living conditions stressful and unhealthy. Utility infrastructures are overloaded, which results in water pressure so low that three or more families must often share one water source. Electrical connections are haphazard and frequently dangerous, and the sewer system frequently overflows, spewing human waste and refuse into the streets. Children have no place to play and are often exposed to diseases caused by exposure to refuse, or from rats or other vermin that eat their flesh while they sleep. High population densities make access for maintenance, repairs, or assistance almost impossible in many parts of Alexandra.

Many of the industrial buildings surrounding Alexandra are in disrepair, empty, or have been illegally occupied by squatters seeking shelter. This a direct reflection of the 40 percent unemployment rate in South Africa, resulting in felony crime climbing to dangerously high levels. Because of the threat of violent crime, many Alexandrans do not leave their houses at night even to go to the bathroom. Hence, wastewater is required to be kept in the house overnight and is disposed of the next day.

On our way to Alexandra, my host tried to prepare me for what I (Deacon Harold) was about to see, but words could not describe my feeling of horror and shock as we made our way to St. Hubert's Church through the streets of Alexandra. In my anxiety, mixed with a bit of Western arrogance, I thought to myself, *What am I doing here?* After we pulled into the heavily fortified parish parking lot, and upon entering the church after being escorted across the street from the rectory, my reason for being there became clear: the church was jam-packed. I was surprised that hundreds of parishioners filled the church on a Thursday night, which, as the pastor later told me, is the typical attendance for each of the Sunday Masses.

Before my talk, the pastor asked me to lead benediction and the Chaplet of Divine Mercy. My feelings of arrogance quickly turned to embarrassment when the African parishioners knew the Latin prayers better than I did. And the singing was some of the most beautiful and meaningful I have ever heard. Materially, these people had nothing, but spiritually, they had everything.

The people of God in Alexandra must completely trust in him alone to sustain them. The spiritual strength that enables them to do this flows from the obedience of faith. This is a faith that sees past the pain and suffering of the physical and material world. It is a faith that inspires and enlivens a people who have nothing to lovingly accept the heavy crosses they have been given, and to see only Jesus, to find comfort and solace in the wounds of the Savior with their gaze fixed upon the radiant and transcendent joy of everlasting life in the world to come.

The people of Alexandra are the very people the Lord came to save, those who live in constant fear and who have nothing to live on but hope. The fact that they live in dire poverty is not by their own choice, but the choice they make to live in voluntary poverty is the absolute realization of their gift from God. This dynamic and vibrant faith comes from a place where those of us who live with a decent roof over our heads and who take the basic necessities of life for granted can never experience or even imagine. The faithful of Alexandra know well that complete trust in the providence of God is born of vulnerability: of not being afraid to break yourself open and pour yourself out in love before the giver of all gifts.

After my talk, a small reception was held in the parish hall. As I made my way into the room, I was quickly surrounded by a group of teens. They asked me how it was possible to live the truth and beauty of our Catholic faith in the midst of such debilitating squalor. Some of them had been exposed to satellite television and were starting to seek hope for the future in the materiality of the Western world.

Like a ray of sunlight reflecting off of a mirror, I tried to focus their attention back to Jesus. I told them that true joy and peace can only come from complete surrender to the will of God. I told them that Western civilization, for the most part, has lost its soul, that she has become the prostitute of the culture of death. I told them that the Lord has great things in store for them if they remain faithful to the truths of the Catholic faith and if they willingly become clay before God, letting his love mold and shape them into the men and women they are called to be.

I told them that when I die, I pray that I will have half the faith that they do, and I encouraged them to continue to live the words of the Gospel and of St. Paul, who beautifully summarizes the spirituality of Alexandra in his letter to the Corinthians: "[The Lord] said to me, 'My grace is sufficient for you, for my power is made perfect in weakness.' I will all the more gladly boast of my weaknesses, that the power of Christ may rest upon me. For the sake of Christ, then, I am content with weaknesses, insults, hardships, persecutions, and calamities; for when I am weak, then I am strong" (2 Corinthians 12:9–10).

Specifically because the township of Alexandra is rooted in a particular place in South Africa, the hearts and souls of its residents are grounded in the love of Christ. Despite severe hardships from years of institutional racism and oppression, the resilient and vibrant community has allowed God's Spirit to flourish within them, bearing the rich fruit of "love, joy, peace, patience, kindness, goodness, faithfulness" (Galatians 5:22). Alexandrans have grown where they were planted, showing us by their example how to "flourish in the courts of our God" (Psalm 92:13).

God knows that places mold and shape us. Just like the Alexandrans are specially sheltered in his love and know him intimately as their consoler, he offers himself to us as both the Lamb of God who takes away the sin of the world, and the Good Shepherd who lays down his life for the sheep. From a land covered in green pastures and rolling in still waters, we are invited to look to our heavenly homeland, to which we are ever being called.

God Prompt—LOVE the Word

Lectio—Listen

> Moses was keeping the flock of his father-in-law Jethro, the priest of Midian; he led his flock beyond the wilderness, and came to Horeb, the mountain of God. There the angel of the Lord appeared to him in a flame of fire out of a bush; he looked, and the bush was blazing, yet it was not consumed. Then Moses said, "I must turn aside and look at this great sight, and see why the bush is not burned up." When the Lord saw that he had turned aside to see, God called to him out of the bush, "Moses, Moses!" And he said, "Here I am." Then he said, "Come no closer! Remove the sandals from your feet, for the place on which you are standing is holy ground." He said further, "I am the God of your father, the God of Abraham, the God of Isaac, and the God of Jacob." And Moses hid his face, for he was afraid to look at God. (Exodus 3:1–6).

Oratio—Observe

Late morning on the shadow side of the distant mountain, the air is already so hot the horizon undulates for miles, when just hours ago the barrenness was so frigid he'd shared breath with huddled animals. He can smell burnt dirt and grass under the harsh odor of either himself or the putrid goats.

Pathetic animals are goats and sheep. Always falling into a crevice or ravine, always running away when you call them, always hungry and thirsty, always head-butting and locking horns, always wandering around in every direction at once, never knowing where they're supposed to go, always bleating for something.

The wide-open silence is so penetrating he hears his fingernails scratching against the woolen-felted skull of an ewe that nuzzles and nibbles against his fingers. He strokes her upturned face.

His stomach growls as the wind blows hot air and sand from a long distance up his flapping tunic and rattles the few dried weeds, but all he feels as he leans against his gnarly staff, looking out over the remote wilderness, is useless. Stupid.

Once the educated, accomplished, prodigious Prince of Egypt, but now exiled. A stinking fugitive goat herder. Named to be a deliverer of his Hebrew people, but washed up now. Finished. Abandoned. Punished. If anyone knows he deserves this grit rather than a silver spoon in his mouth, it's him.

He's been out here in the desolate places of Mount Horeb, on the run, for forty years, the could've-beens replaying over and over in his mind. People used to bow to him. But now, not even the sheep hear his voice. There's nothing left of that life. It's all been completely stripped down, cut off, and removed out here in the desolation.

Ah, well, the same acute sense of righteousness that once provoked him to murder assures him he deserves this life-sentence. "If you can't run with Pharaoh's chariots, then get yourself to the desert," is his attitude as he catches sight of a flame leaping up out of the distant heatwaves.

Is the sand on fire? he thinks, and then feels stupid again. There's not enough vegetation to burn. But it's definitely fire. Must be a dittany shrub. Those scraggly bushes burn themselves out in a minute's puff, so his attention wanders. He watches without seeing it, and wonders about his mothers back in Egypt, one his Hebrew birth mother, the other his Egyptian adoptive mother. Is she ashamed? Angry? Alive? He stabs the staff into the dirt and kicks at the dust he raised. Where is the God of Abraham, Isaac, and Jacob out in this forsaken wilderness, this vast open sky, this yawning abyss? Where? Nowhere.

He turns to collect the animals and herd them to shelter for the evening, but the light from the fire is oddly brighter in the growing gloom, and a shiver warns him when he still sees the clear outline of stems and stubby leaves inside its distant glow. Intrigued now, he peers through the rosemary-scented cloud of smoke blowing over him in the wind. His steps quicken as he hurries to investigate, and he is utterly horrified when a disembodied voice flares out from the crackling flames and erupts in a burst of popping light that burns through him with its terrible snapping sound: "Moses."

As though Moses had earlier spoken his thought aloud, the blazing bush thunders, "I AM the God of Abraham, Isaac, and Jacob," as he calls him out of the desert to the salvation Moses was named and had been preparing for all along.

Meditatio—Verbalize

Dear Jesus, forgive me for believing I could run from my sin. I pretended that you did not see me and expected no one would know, but it has separated me from what I love and exiled me to a lonely barren land.

Today, help me to cooperate with my desert surroundings to do away with all the trappings of sinful Egypt that crowd and drown and suffocate your work in me and deceive me into thinking I am where you are. Help me to hear your voice in my desolations, so I can encounter you on a level that will transform me forever.

Like Moses, I know what failure feels like. But I also want to experience you, to hear you speak in that fire and flame, to remove my shoes in awe, and leave your presence ready to change the world. Please call me forward, Lord, to where you are, be it desert loneliness or barren wilderness. I am at the foot of the desolate mountain, wandering around, killing time, awkwardly groping for you. And as you summon me, make me know in my depths that even while I ran from my guilt, you were already waiting for me in the desert.

Contemplatio—Entrust
Perhaps you want to rest your little woolen head in the Good Shepherd's lap and let him hold you tight, or reflect on how you can be a better shepherd to serve, protect, and defend your family and the Church against the wolves and hirelings of the culture.

chapter five

The When of the Bible

The Easter I (Sonja) was received into full communion with the Church was utterly wondrous for me. I remember thinking that somehow I had never, in my thirty-something years, properly celebrated the season before.

I spent the whole Lent leading up to it in quiet. I gave up coffee. I meditated on the Sorrowful Mysteries of the rosary every day. I watched *The Passion*. I did the Way of the Cross. I attended every Holy Week Mass that was available. I couldn't *wait* to receive my first Eucharist and become one in communion with all my new brothers and sisters, but I loved the agony of waiting too, because it made me long to be one with Jesus all the more.

At Easter Vigil I bawled like a baby through the whole thing. I went back the next morning, just so I could do it all again, sing it all again, read it all again, receive it all again, to say, "He is risen, *indeed!*" again. I was so excited that it would be Easter for fifty whole days!

I had lived through three decades of Easters without that intensity of participation. I don't think I had ever really experienced, before that, what it was *really* all about. Although not with the same zeal as that first year, I still love getting into the Lenten zone every year. What makes all the difference for me? It's the Church's liturgical calendar, the "when" of the Bible.

As a non-Catholic, the word *liturgy* was foreign to me, but liturgy (from the Greek word *leitourgia* meaning "a work of the people") simply means a public worship ceremony or a ritual. The liturgical calendar, then (in its widest application), is the formal yearly cycle of feast days that characterizes communal Christian worship.

Spiral Stairway to Heaven

Pagan religions (think of the Egyptians) saw time as an endless cycle, and still do. By ordaining their observance of this sacred schedule of holy, festive days of obligation centered around the tabernacle, God was teaching his people that time was created with a definite beginning and a definite end, and to acknowledge him as the Lord of their time—of *all* time and history. They were meant to learn through its schedule that God draws close to us, he lives and works, in space and time. By his providence, all times and seasons are ordered. He invites us to live and work with him. How exciting!

So, rather than a timeline, we'd like you to begin thinking of time as a spiral moving ever forward, upward, and toward the Day of Judgment. The liturgical year lends itself to this view, so that like the Israelites, thinking of the year and time in general as a spiraling wheel will give you a good sense of sacred time.

Within our spiraling, big-picture sense of history, Catholics also experience the passing of seasons, days, and hours as repeating cycles of meditations on the sacred mysteries of Christ. Like the Old Testament Israelites, Catholics relive the action of God in history every single year through the liturgical year. We re-present the Gospel from Christ's incarnation and birth to his passion, ascension, and reign.

In the spring, he enters the world in Mary's immaculate womb; in the winter, he is born, circumcised, and named. He is raised in the Holy Family, and meets his cousin John. He goes into the desert, and we go with him during Lent. We follow him through his passion, which is soon vanquished by his resurrection, ascension, and Pentecost. Now he reigns, and we await his Second Coming as we prepare to celebrate again his First Coming. Then the cycle begins again, like a wheel that's been spinning for two millennia. When we participate in this spiral of remembrance and anticipation by celebrating the feasts of the Church, we draw intimately close to God in time and history.

The Church is so wise to lead us into periods of intense, deliberate preparation through the seasons of Advent and Lent. These penitential times make our joyful celebrations of the baby King and his resurrection more significant. More thoughtful. More meaningful. Whose great idea was the liturgical year? It was God's.

KEEPING TIME WITH GOD

Time and space are creations of God. They are the framework through which humans accumulate sensory data for growth, knowledge, and learning. God created the cosmos on a defined schedule. It was an object lesson of exact law, exact plan, exact order, and exact method. Six days of work, carefully planned, scheduled, and completed were followed by rest. Whether we accept the story as literal or figurative matters less than learning the lesson in timekeeping that creation teaches, because all of time and history is based and builds on that first week.

Later, on a seasonal and annual basis, God specified more exactly how he wanted his people to keep time with him by giving them special feast days that revolved around the tabernacle. These special celebrations helped remind the people of important events in their history with God. Feast days included rest, offerings, and a sacred assembly.

"From the time of the Mosaic law, the People of God have observed fixed feasts, beginning with Passover, to commemorate the astonishing actions of the Savior God, to give him thanks for them, to perpetuate their remembrance, and to teach new generations to conform their conduct to them" (*CCC,* 1164). In addition to a tabernacle, solemn ceremonies, and vivid rituals, proper worship was meant to include a liturgical schedule.

In Leviticus 23, the chapter and paragraph headings in bold print offer a convenient list of the major feasts. There were other sacred times in the Old Testament liturgical year, but the major festivals were the Sabbath, Passover, Unleavened Bread, First Fruits, Weeks, Trumpets, Day of Atonement, and Booths Festivals. Old Testament feasts are fascinating because all of time and history is and will be based on their template.

THE ANGELUS

One of my favorite meditations on sacred time is of Millet's painting *The Angelus*. I (Sonja) can almost see and hear the church bells ringing down the lane to remind us all to take a bit of refreshment, a little cleansing breath, and pray on the sixes and twelves of every day. I bought an antique mantel clock just to hear it chime and to consider how many people prayed, and still pray, on the hour. I can almost feel the sense of reverence for morning, noon, and evening, marked by the bells, the brief respite, and the prayers. Can't you?

God is all-wise. He knows and commands what we need. We need rest. We're talking about a principle we might wish were different, but we will not be the ones for whom the ancient rules change.

A SACRED REST

The Sabbath was a weekly time of gathering, offerings, worship, and rest. The word *Sabbath* means "rest." "You shall keep the Sabbath, for it is holy to you.… Work shall be done for six days, but the seventh is the Sabbath of rest, holy to the Lord. It is a sign forever between me and the people of Israel that in six days the Lord made heaven and earth, and on the seventh day he rested, and was refreshed'" (Exodus 31:14–17).

God rested. The Sabbath worship-rest was a deliberate act of inter-ference, an interruption of the work week—a decree of no-work. Isn't that refreshing? The word *rest* makes us think of mountain streams, a hammock and book, and long Sunday naps. What images does the word *rest* bring to your mind?

The children of Israel were to keep the Sabbath as a perpetual covenant. When the Bible talks about the Sabbath, it remembers creation, when God worked for six days and rested on the seventh. In Deuteronomy 5:15 we find that God specifically tied the Sabbath to redemption. In Exodus 31:17 we see the Sabbath "sign" was supposed to be observed "forever."

The Sabbath was a time set aside each week, every Saturday, to recall God's work and rest in creation, and his rescuing action on behalf of the people from Egyptian slavery. At the end of a grueling work week, the Sabbath was…a luxury? Boring rule? In Mark 2:27, Jesus says the Sabbath was made for man, not man for Sabbath keeping: the Sabbath was a gift.

We are not Jewish; we are Christian. Today, we no longer keep the Sabbath: "I was in the Spirit on the Lord's day" (Revelation 1:10). We keep the Lord's day, as the apostles called it. We observe the Lord's day on Sunday after them and according to their authority, because it's the day Jesus completed his work on the cross and rose from the dead. It is the eighth day, or the first day of the New Creation wrought in Christ. Even now, God is always working, yet always at rest.

We study and observe Sunday, because "Sunday is the foundation and kernel of the whole liturgical year" (*CCC*, 1193). "Sunday fulfills the spiritual truth of the Jewish sabbath and announces man's eternal rest in God. The sabbath, which represented the completion of the first creation, has been replaced by Sunday, which recalls the new creation inaugurated by the Resurrection of Christ" (*CCC*, 2175, 2190).

Sunday replaces and carries forward the Old Testament Sabbath by fulfilling the rhythm and spirit of God's command to worship and rest every week. It is similar to the Sabbath but not the same. Our perpetual, weekly observance includes rest, worship, and remembrance of God's saving actions on our behalf in Christ. Each week our daily work continues God's work in history and creation. Therefore, like him, we also rest.

Rest is both physical and spiritual. Sunday and work are not opposites; they complement one another. Sunday is the happy crown of our work week.

Our Sunday reflects the Sabbath feast, a day of obligation that includes worship and rest so that part of worship *is rest* and part of rest *is worship*. Have you ever thought of rest and worship as so interrelated? Does this thought change your perception of Sunday worship at all?

God uses the workplaces of our daily lives as a primary tool for our spiritual formation. Sunday reorients us to what God is doing, rather than what we have been doing. The interruption of work that Sunday gives us time to consider how God has worked in us and through us in the past week. Recalling Jesus's work of the cross, we can participate in that supreme work by receiving the Eucharist, and by offering our own duties and labors in communion with his. Even if we must work on Sunday, like our pastors do, Sunday worship remains an obligation. We can, and should, always set aside another day every week for rest.

The Old Testament Sabbath feast was the basis of the Old Testament liturgical year, establishing a weekly day of obligation that included rest, worship, and remembrance. In Jewish thought, the Sabbath teachings in the Old Testament Law were prophetic of the Messianic kingdom. The Sabbath foreshadowed our own Sunday and points us toward that final, Messianic, Promised Land of rest. As we saw in the last chapter, there remains another, different rest for God's people at the end of the ages, one in which we will no longer labor.

God is very interested in our rest-worship-gathering, enough to emphasize it in the Scriptures over and over:

> Blessed is the man who does this, and the son of man who holds it fast, who keeps the sabbath, not profaning it, and keeps his hand from doing any evil. (Isaiah 56:2)

> If you turn back your foot from the sabbath, from doing your pleasure on my holy day, and call the sabbath a delight and the holy day of the Lord honorable; if you honor it, not going your own ways, or seeking your own pleasure, or talking idly; then you shall take delight in the Lord, and I will make you ride upon the heights of the earth; I will feed you with the heritage of Jacob your father, for the mouth of the Lord has spoken. (Isaiah 58:13–14)

> For thus said the Lord God, the Holy One of Israel, "In returning and rest you shall be saved; in quietness and in trust shall be your strength." (Isaiah 30:15)

> Moreover I swore to them in the wilderness that I would not bring them into the land which I had given them, a land flowing with milk and honey, the most glorious of all lands, because they rejected my ordinances and did not walk in my statutes, and profaned my sabbaths; for their heart went after their idols. (Ezekiel 20:15)

Over and over in Ezekiel 20 it is said we shall live by keeping the Sabbath holy and that we cannot live without it. Perhaps the reason is because the worship-rest of the Sabbath is absolutely necessary to human well-being. We included a few, but rest assured the Bible is chock-full of promises and warnings regarding Sabbath keeping.

The Sabbath foreshadowed our own Sunday. "The Sunday celebration of the Lord's Day and his Eucharist is at the heart of the Church's life. 'Sunday is the day on which the paschal mystery is celebrated in light of apostolic tradition and is to be observed as the foremost holy day of obligation in the universal Church'" (*CCC*, 2177).

An Involuntary Sabbatical

When God began teaching me (Sonja) this principle, I resisted it wholeheartedly. I had too much to do. I had also been laid off, professionally, and had rested enough in my estimation. I was itching to *do something*! But God kept me on the shelf until I really, truly began to practice this discipline, for myself and my family.

It took me and my body a couple of months to figure out the ancient rhythm, but then I wallowed in it like a piglet in a mud puddle. To this day, I schedule my time and travel, very strictly and whenever possible, so that I do nothing on Sundays but teach religion classes and go to Mass. The laundry is done on Saturday or waits till Monday. I nap. I watch period movies or British TV. Every week.

No one does dishes. Everyone plays and rests. We take bike rides and walks together in the afternoon. I give my kids a free hour of video-game time, just to make Sunday a celebration for them too. Beloved, for the good of your soul, your sanity, and your dear family, we want you to begin guarding your Sundays. What can you do ahead of time, during the week, to free up your Sundays for church and family?

The First Festival Octave, a Weeklong Sabbath

In addition to one day a week, God's saving action in delivering his people from Egyptian slavery was so important that it required a whole week's observance. Sort of a long Sabbath, the annual Feasts of Passover and Unleavened Bread reminded the people of God's special care for them. Initially, God sent Moses to ask Pharaoh to let the Hebrew slaves to go to Mount Sinai to worship him. Pharaoh said no. God warned Pharaoh, through Moses, that he would make

Egypt wish otherwise through plagues if he did not relent and let his people go. The last, most devastating of those plagues was the death of every firstborn of both man and beast in the kingdom.

The original Passover story is in Exodus 12 (remember that both *exodus* and *Moses* mean "drawn out," or "leaving"). It was spring, March or early April. To protect them from the plague of the firstborn, the Hebrew people were told to kill a sacrificial spring lamb and splash its blood on their doorposts (see Exodus 12:13). The blood of the lamb was necessary because when the death angel went through the Egyptian kingdom to administer the plague of death on every firstborn, he would "pass over" all the homes that had the sign of lamb's blood on the doorposts.

That same night, they were to roast the lamb and eat it with unleavened bread in what would become an annual Hebrew communal meal. Their bread had to be unleavened because they were in a hurry (Exodus 12:11). God delivered them, that first Passover, in such a quick and miraculous way that they had no time to make preparations or wait for their bread to rise. Later, leaven became symbolic of sin in the Scriptures, as though to say on our journey home to heaven we have no time to allow sin to ferment and take over our lives.

Like the Sabbath, the Passover feast was supposed to be observed forever. "This day shall be for you a memorial day, and you shall keep it as a feast to the Lord; throughout your generations you shall observe it as an ordinance" (Exodus 12:14). The children of Israel were to keep the Passover as a perpetual covenant.

God's people kept the Passover feast all the way to Jesus's time, at which point it was necessary to change it a bit, because he is the new Passover, the Paschal Lamb, in his person. We see in John 1:29 that John the Baptist calls Jesus the Lamb (*pasch*) of God who takes away the sin of the world. Jesus is the fulfillment of all those many years of Old Testament sacrificial lambs.

The Passover lamb removed the judgment of death from the Hebrew people during the first old covenant Passover, and they commemorated that event throughout their history. Jesus, the Lamb of God, established a new covenant and a new Passover that would remove the *eternal* judgment of disobedience and sin from us. "Now as they were eating, Jesus took bread, and blessed, and broke it, and gave it to the disciples and said, 'Take, eat; this is my body.' And he took a cup, and when he had given thanks he gave it to them, saying, 'Drink of it, all of you; for this is my blood of the covenant, which is poured out for many for the forgiveness of sins'" (Matthew 26:26–28).

Jesus's words are an almost exact repeat of his earlier, preparatory teachings in John 6. "So Jesus said to them, 'Truly, truly, I say to you, unless you eat the flesh of the Son of man and drink his blood, you have no life in you; he who eats my flesh and drinks my blood has eternal life, and I will raise him up at the last day. For my flesh is food indeed, and my blood is drink indeed. He who eats my flesh and drinks my blood abides in me, and I in him'" (John 6:53–56).

The apostles were supposed to eat his body and drink his blood, and as often as they did, the effect of the covenant would be the forgiveness of sins (Matthew 26:28). Not by accident, Jesus instituted the Eucharist and was crucified as the sacrificial Lamb of God on the Jewish Feasts of Unleavened Bread and Passover. Unlike the Passover lambs whose blood caused the death angel to simply pass over God's people, Jesus's blood actually takes away the sin of the world, fulfilling these old covenant feasts in his own Body and Blood, so that they remain forever.

Similarly to the old covenant Jews, we eat the Lamb. His blood is then applied to the doorposts of our hearts, saving us from the eternal consequences of sin. Oh, how this truth makes our hearts soar! Keeping this new Passover feast, the Eucharist, draws the Lamb into our hearts to dwell. Jesus comes to tabernacle with us through the Eucharist we celebrate every Sunday and every Easter. Because of this, Sunday is often called a "little Easter."

The Old Testament Passover was fulfilled in Christ, who is our Passover. St. Paul tells us in 1 Corinthians 5:7–8, "For our Passover has been sacrificed, that is, Christ; therefore, let us keep the feast." This is important, because some Christians believe all feasts have been eliminated. St. Paul says otherwise. The Bible commands us to keep the feast. Catholics keep the new covenant Passover feast— Easter. We do this daily and weekly at Mass, and annually at Easter, along with our other liturgical celebrations.

> In the age of the Church, between the Passover of Christ already accomplished once for all, and its consummation in the kingdom of God, the liturgy celebrated on fixed days bears the imprint of the newness of the mystery of Christ. (*CCC*, 1164)

LORD OF THE SEASONS

A country girl, I (Sonja) grew up in the South, where corn and tomatoes and beans are what you live and breathe in August. When my husband and I were first married, we planted a nominal vegetable garden—a few tomatoes, a couple rows of corn, a bean plant or so. That year, we made an unexpected trip abroad on mission. The vegetable garden was neglected in favor of fundraising, planning, and preparations for the trip.

When we returned from Europe at the end of September, the garden was a jungle of weeds taller than I. It was dry and unkempt and had sprawled all out into the yard. But there was all this *fruit*! I was astounded. We hadn't watered. We hadn't weeded. We hadn't had time to do anything to it at all. While there wasn't a bumper crop, there was far more fruit than we could eat. I was captivated by the miracle of poking a single dead seed into dark swaddling earth and returning a couple months later to more nourishment and life than we could even manage to eat.

For every rural farming people, harvest time has always been a time of great celebration and fun. God instructed his people to keep him in mind at harvest time through special festivals. They were to cease from work, gather at the tabernacle, and present offerings of thanksgiving to him, the Lord of the Harvest.

In the Old Testament, the Feast of Weeks was one such celebration, also known by a name more familiar to us: Pentecost. The term *weeks* illustrated seven weeks of seven days. That's forty-nine days, plus the one on which the feast began, equaling fifty. Therefore Pentecost was a two-month-or-so festival that got its name from the Greek for fifty. Pentecost formally began with the one-day Feast of Firstfruits. The two feasts were quickly combined into one, however, so we will look at them together.

Leviticus 23:9–22 shows us that the Feasts of Firstfruits and Pentecost were, together, a religious celebration of the grain harvest. Before the people could eat any of the grain of a new harvest, they were to bring a bundle to the tabernacle in proportion to how much God had blessed them that year. The priest would wave, or elevate, the offerings before God as a gift of thanksgiving. The offering was a little like a thanksgiving tithe, right off the top, and it acknowledged their reliance on God's faithful provision of the harvest. It was also an expectation that God would give the rest of the harvest as his continued blessing. Like the others, these feasts were to last "forever" (Leviticus 29:14, 21).

While we are not Jewish and do not keep the Jewish Law or feasts, we are Christian. The Jews looked forward, anticipating the coming Christ. Christians look backward to his first advent, passion, resurrection, and ascension. Christians keep the law of love which Jesus commanded (Romans 13:8–10). This law includes the feasts that help us love and remember the sacred occasions upon which Christianity is built. They keep us in time with God in a similar way to that of the former liturgical feasts.

The Feast of Pentecost informally began with Firstfruits, but while at Firstfruits whole stalks of grain were waved before Lord in the tabernacle, at Pentecost they were ground into flour and baked into loaves to offer to him with gifts of wine (Leviticus 23:15–22). For the Jews, Pentecost also commemorated the giving of the Law on Mount Sinai which later Jewish rabbis purport to have happened fifty days after leaving Egypt (Exodus 19:1–2).[1]

It was with this feast schedule context in mind that Jesus, a faithful Jew, gave his disciples careful instructions in Acts 1:4–8 immediately after his resurrection, telling them to "wait for the promise of the Father," the Holy Spirit. "When the day of Pentecost had come, they were all together in one place. And suddenly a sound came from heaven like the rush of a mighty wind, and it filled all the house where they were sitting. And there appeared to them tongues as of fire, distributed and resting on each one of them. And they were all filled with the Holy Spirit and began to speak in other tongues, as the Spirit gave them utterance" (Acts 2:1–4).

Remember in the Old Testament the Feast of Pentecost actually began with the one-day Feast of Firstfruits. St. Paul uses the term "firstfruits" in 1 Corinthians 15:17–23 to refer to the resurrection of Christ as the "firstfruits" from the dead. The Old Testament Feast of Firstfruits corresponds with the New Testament resurrection of Christ, the "firstfruit" of the bodily resurrection. If he is the "first-fruit," we are the fruit that follows. Can you see, now, why we say this in the Creed and at every Mass? "I believe in the holy Catholic Church, the communion of saints, the forgiveness of sins, the resurrection of the body."

Jesus draws a connection between himself and a seed, saying the seed is somehow "glorified" by dying, because in doing so, it produces a great harvest. "And Jesus answered them, 'The hour has come for the Son of man to be glorified. Truly, truly, I say to you, unless a grain of wheat falls into the earth and dies, it remains alone; but if it dies, it bears much fruit'" (John 12:23–24).

THE BIRTHDAY OF THE CHURCH

I (Sonja) remember my youngest son's birthday very vividly. I had a C-section with my first child, so when I became pregnant during the nine-month waiting period for maternity coverage following my husband's job change, I panicked. I asked God, "What in the *world* are you doing?" I knew an out-of-pocket $20,000 hospital bill for another C-section was inevitable, and I couldn't figure out why he hadn't blessed us with another baby *after* our medical insurance would actually cover the expense of delivery. I remember pouring out my worries to him during morning prayer, and that the answer was so gentle: "Sonja, this baby is a gift." *Yeah, yeah. I know all the verses about children being gifts from God and all that*, I thought.

So when my little one came into the world in less than two hours, too quickly for a C-section, epidural, or even pain meds, and on my own birthday, I had to chuckle a little at God's extraordinary sense of humor. A very personal, very deliberate, very miraculous birthday present!

Pentecost is sometimes called the birthday of the Church, and the gift the Church received was the Holy Spirit. The disciples listened to Jesus's instructions and waited prayerfully after his ascension. On a feast ripe with the promise of harvest and the remembrance of Sinai, the Holy Spirit fell upon them as a loud, visible, life-giving "power from on high." That particular Pentecost was the day of firstfruits of the Church, the beginning of the great harvest of souls that would become the new people of God through the Holy Spirit.

That Pentecost, a new people of God was born of the spiritual fertility of the third person of the Trinity, as St. Jerome poetically remembers. "There is Sinai, here Zion; there the trembling mountain, here the trembling house; there the flaming mountain, here the flaming tongues; there the noisy thunderings, here the sounds of many tongues; there the clangor of the rams horn, here the notes of the gospel-trumpet."[2]

A YEAR OF CELEBRATIONS

In this chapter's emphasis on the "when" of the Bible and the liturgical worship schedule surrounding the tabernacle, we couldn't begin to cover all the interesting feasts and their particular contributions to the lives and worship of God's people, Old and New Testament. Instead, we focused on three of the major festivals that are obviously and immediately applicable to our Catholic life right now. To wrap up our discussion, we will hit the highlights of those that remain, because the Old Testament liturgical schedule was something of a repeating pattern, or template, for all of religious history and time.

God must have wanted his people to be celebrating all the time, because there were more feasts throughout the year. The next feast in the Old Testament calendar was the Feast of Trumpets. For the Old Testament people, there were at least two ways of calculating the year. The religious year regulated the annual cycle of festivals and began in the spring with Passover. The Feast of Trumpets signaled the beginning of the civil new year in the autumn, and is still Jewish practice today.

The Catholic religious year begins at Advent, meaning "coming," but most of us also celebrate some sort of secular New Year, too. If you notice, Advent begins and ends with readings on the First and Second Comings of Christ. The Feast of Trumpets is sometimes said to anticipate the New Creation inaugurated by the Second Coming. Can you guess why? "For the Lord himself will descend from heaven with a cry of command, with the archangel's call, and with the sound of the trumpet of God. And the dead in Christ will rise first; then we who are alive, who are left, shall be caught up together with them in the clouds to meet the Lord in the air; and so we shall always be with the Lord" (1 Thessalonians 4:16–17).

Deacon Harold and I get the biggest thrill anticipating what the Second Coming will be like. Did you realize we will all be with Jesus when he returns to earth? We look forward to the final trumpet that will call us to resurrection and home!

The Day of Atonement was another important feast, the high holy day and "day of all days" in the Jewish religious year, because complete atonement, meaning satisfaction, was made for the sin of whole nation. It is pictured most accurately now in the passion and death of Christ, and the loving reconciliation with God that all people are offered through him. Jesus is our "day of atonement." It was a season of solemn fasting and penance (Leviticus 23:26–32) that anticipated the seasons of fasting and penance that precede our own two holiest holy days, the nativity and resurrection of Christ.

Finally, the Feast of Booths, or Tabernacles, reminds us that God always provides for us while we are on this pilgrimage of wilderness wandering on our way to the Promised Land. "To thee do we send up our sighs, mourning, and weeping in this valley of tears." It was sometimes called the Feast of Tabernacles, because God instructed the people to make themselves lean-tos out of branches and camp outside in them for a week in remembrance of their journey through the wilderness (Leviticus 23:39–42).

The feasts had both an immediate agricultural significance, and they commemorated national events of God's people. Through the Church, we see that this is still true. God fulfilled and carried forward the old feasts and festivals into the Church and time through Christ, so that they remained perpetual as he commanded all those millennia ago. We know that keeping Christian feasts is really a participation of the heavenly celebration occurring as we speak, and anticipation of the final celebration of Christ's union with the Church at the Wedding Feast of the Lamb and end of history. We find that a comforting meditation.

Liturgy is the official divine worship of the Church (*CCC,* 1163–1171). It takes place within a liturgical calendar. As I (Sonja) shared earlier in the chapter, I dearly love the liturgical calendar, especially because it was God's idea. The overarching point of this schedule is that we both remember salvation past and anticipate salvation future. Because of this huge sweep of salvation remembrance and anticipation, the liturgical calendar is not a bunch of random days that require us to go to Mass, often give us days off, and offer fun family traditions and happy songs. No one makes or invents liturgical worship. Like Christmas, which was not celebrated until about AD 360, our liturgical calendar is something living that grew from the root of Christ over many millennia of faith.

The Old Testament liturgical schedule was established by God and centered around the tabernacle, foreshadowing our Church's liturgical year. The Church's feast days are days of obligation, like those of the Old Testament, that include rest, worship, offerings, and gathering of God's people. Isn't it marvelous that through our holy days, especially Sunday and Easter, we participate in the heavenly celebration occurring right now? At Mass, especially, we connect with the angels and the saints who are already celebrating in heaven.

By keeping time with God through the liturgical year the Church on earth shows that she is united with the liturgy of heaven. How wonderful that our liturgical calendar points us to heaven in which we will ultimately worship in communion forever with Jesus. Amen! It was this sense of connectedness to past, present, and future saints that made my first Easter as a Catholic so meaningful to me. Even now, the Catholic liturgical calendar keeps us all joined to the communion and celebrations occurring in heaven.

"From the time of the Mosaic law, the People of God have observed fixed feasts, beginning with Passover, to commemorate the astonishing actions of the Savior God, to give him thanks for them, to perpetuate their remembrance, and to teach new generations to conform their conduct to them.

"In the age of the Church, between the Passover of Christ already accomplished once for all, and its consummation in the kingdom of God, the liturgy celebrated on fixed days bears the imprint of the newness of the mystery of Christ" (*CCC,* 1164).

Let's Review

This is the "when" of the Bible.

- *We keep time with God through a liturgical calendar,* as he prescribed.
- *The Old Testament liturgical schedule of feast days is the template* for all of time and history.
- Biblical and secular events often seem like two different chronicles, but *"regular" history and "religious" history are not two separate things. It's all one history.* The chronology of secular history and liturgical worship wind around each other as one timeline.
- *The liturgical year establishes us all in God's "when."*
- *The Old Testament Sabbath corresponds to the New Testament Sunday.*
- *The Sabbath teaches us* that part of worship is rest, and part of rest is worship.
- *Sunday is the foundation* and kernel of the whole liturgical year.
- *Old Testament Passover corresponds to New Testament Easter,* our "Great Sunday" and the highest holy day of the Christian year.

Invitation

As brothers and sisters of Christ by baptism, we participate in the work of Christ at every Mass, instituted by Jesus at the Last Supper. "The cup of blessing which we bless, is it not a participation in the blood of Christ? The bread which we break, is it not a participation in the body of Christ?" (1 Corinthians 10:16). In fact, remember the word *liturgy* comes from the Greek word *leitourgía* that means "a work of the people." How does our participation at Mass enable us to live a Eucharistic faith every day? The key can be found in Jesus's own words: "Do this in remembrance of me" (Luke 22:19 and 1 Corinthians 11:24).

The word *remembrance*, as Christ uses it, does not mean "to remember the past" in the way you recall something that happened previously in your life, like your last birthday. "Remembrance" (*anamnesis* in Greek and *zakhar* in Hebrew) is sacrificial language referring to the sweet-smelling smoke of incense offered with a sacrifice of grain, wine, and oil, specifically, a memorial sacrifice offered in atonement for the sins of the past (see Leviticus 2:16; 5:12; 6:8; 24:7; and Numbers 5:26). This is the work that Jesus did on the cross that produced an abundance of graces and blessings for the world. This is the work that Jesus entrusted to his Apostles at the Last Supper and that we participate in at every liturgy.

This is not a difficult idea to grasp once you understand the connection between the Last Supper and the Jewish Passover, the night where the people of Israel were freed from slavery in Egypt. The Feast of Passover is still celebrated every year by the Jews and "was a night of watching by the Lord, to bring them out of the land of Egypt...this same night is a night of watching kept to the Lord by all the people of Israel throughout their generations" (Exodus 12:42).

In the Jewish way of thinking,

Biblical history is not merely the recording of random events in the life of the people of Israel; instead, "it is history as the arena of God's activity." This view of history is obviously distinct from our modern concern with the recording of human events that are recorded down to the most minor details, but…"the historical acts by which [the Lord] founded the community of Israel were absolute."

Because these events were understood to be absolute in nature, "they did not share the fate of all other events, which inevitably slip back into the past"; instead, "they [are] actual for each subsequent generation"; and this not just in the sense of furnishing the imagination with a vivid present picture of past events—no, it [is] only the community assembled for a festival that by recitation and ritual brought Israel…"really and truly into the historic situation to which the festival in question was related."[3]

In other words, the Passover that is celebrated today is not simply a remembrance of an important event that happened in Jewish history thousands of years ago. They are actually there, in Egypt, through remembrance or re-participation.

The same is true for us at Mass. We are not simply remembering what Jesus did on Calvary over two thousand years ago. We are actually standing at the foot of the cross, and the very same graces and blessings that flowed from the cross are made real and present for us in the Eucharist. The Eucharistic Christ gives us the gift of his Body, Blood, soul, and divinity so that, when we cooperate with the grace we receive in the Blessed Sacrament, we are enabled and empowered to live in the freedom of God's will.

This is why Sunday is the Lord's day. This is the day we, as a family united in prayer, collectively remember and receive the awesome power of God's love for us. This is the day where we set aside all of the cares and worries of the world, and rest in the Lord—basking in God's love and mercy that is without end. This is the day where we remember what is really important in life, and where we take time to recharge our minds and bodies for the work ahead of us in the coming week. "This is the day the Lord has made, let us rejoice and be glad" (Psalm 118:24).

GOD PROMPT—LOVE THE WORD

Lectio—Listen

> For I received from the Lord what I also delivered to you, that the Lord Jesus on the night when he was betrayed took bread, and when he had given thanks, he broke it, and said, "This is my body which is for you. Do this in remembrance of me."
>
> In the same way also the cup, after supper, saying, "This cup is the new covenant in my blood. Do this, as often as you drink it, in remembrance of me."
>
> For as often as you eat this bread and drink the cup, you proclaim the Lord's death until he comes. Whoever, therefore, eats the bread or drinks the cup of the Lord in an unworthy manner will be guilty of profaning the body and blood of the Lord. (1 Corinthians 11:23–27)

Oratio—Observe

Reread the passage, imagining you are present with the disciples when Jesus says these miraculous words.

Is it daylight outside, or has darkness closed in around the flickering lamp light in the room? Can you hear street noise, or is it quiet but for the breathing or laughter or discussion of your companions? What was the last bite you took; what are you chewing? How do you feel as you see young John reclining against Jesus's chest and Judas laughing nervously with the disciple beside him? Is it you who speaks with Judas, unaware of his duplicity? What happens around the table when Jesus surprises everyone with his sudden change in the ancient Passover ritual?

Does he look into your eyes when he hands you the hunk of bread? Is it warm? Can you smell the smoke from the outdoor oven on it? Is it crusty on the outside or soft? What does he mean, "This is my body given up for you"? How will he be broken and spilled out like the bread and wine he offers you at this, his very last meal?

Meditatio—Verbalize

Lord, how do I look into your eyes and receive this bread and chalice from your hand while remembering you are about to be beaten, spit on, flogged, and hung by nails on that terrifying instrument of torture for me? How do I chew and swallow this bread, knowing your body was broken in pieces, and consume this tangy wine, knowing it is the blood that poured out of your veins? How can you also give me your *body* and *blood* as nourishment when you have already given all you had on the cross? It is too high for me to grasp, this love you extend to me every day, every week, every year of my life. I do not deserve it. I thank you for your matchless sacrifice and kneel at your feet, overwhelmed in love. I receive you. My heart is open, and I receive.

Contemplatio—Entrust

Maybe you'd like to relax against his bosom for a few moments, like John, before Jesus leaves to be crucified for you.

chapter six

The How of the Old Testament

As a former non-Catholic, I (Sonja) always wondered why God would go to such trouble to prepare his Old Testament people for the Church in Christ if it wasn't supposed to be anything like what they had known in the Old Testament. So it was, partly, the connections between the Old Testament tabernacle and the Catholic Church that drew me into Catholicism. Catholic trappings, rituals, and practices may seem old-fashioned, outdated, or even unbiblical. But Catholic worship and practice is prescribed by God himself, scripturally rooted in the Old Testament tabernacle, modeled after the worship occurring in heaven right now, and reflected in the individual soul.

We know what kind of worship pleases God because, through the Old Testament tabernacle, he specified for us what it should look like. Because Old Testament worship was modeled after heavenly worship, we see that proper New Testament worship should also follow the tabernacle's structure and order.

The revelation of God's desire for worship is contained in the Pentateuch. In these first five books, God revealed his will directly to the people: how they were to behave, worship, and live in the closest possible connection to him.

This law goes way back, about 1440 BC or so, but it is important because through it, we can discern some wonderful things about *how* our unchangeable, consistent God interacts with his people, even today. Tabernacle worship is the "how" of the Old Testament.

Called to the Mountain

In Exodus 3:18, we read that God sent Moses to Pharaoh because he wanted Pharaoh to allow the people to take a three-day leave of absence of sorts, so they could offer sacrifices of worship to him.

The next several chapters of Exodus are the story of Moses's repeated confrontations with a stubborn Pharaoh. Ultimately, because he would not allow the people to worship God for a few days, God removed them from Pharaoh's rule completely. Consider that if you're in a job that requires you to work on Sunday. Maybe you want to ask God to intervene on your behalf. He'll provide for you, just like he did the Israelites.

Finally, they made it out. In Exodus 19:1–2 we find they made a pit stop on the way to the Promised Land at a mountain, the mountain of God. I (Sonja) love this thought.

We live a state away from my family, and every time we go home, we drive through the Blue Ridge Mountains. On our scenic route through Tennessee and North Carolina, there's an overlook where we stop every trip. It's the oddest lookout I've ever seen because it doesn't offer the panoramic view of the tops of the misty, blue mountains that most lookouts do. It's more of a mountain-in-your-face thing.

I always climb the rock wall that protects tourists from falling down the side into the gorge below and stand on its surface with my arms thrown wide. It's not something I would ever allow my kids to do, but it produces *the* most spectacular effect. Without the rock wall, or anything else at all, to restrict the view, the whole side of the mountain is in my face. I have to throw my head way back to see the top of it. Straight ahead, all there is to see from this perch is the vast, green face of God.

He looks me in the eye.

His breath smells like earth, fir, and pine, and his voice swirls in a whisper of misty fog around my body. It leaves me breathless. Every. Single. Time.

The Bible is full of this type of mountain imagery for God. It's not surprising at all, then, that God would call his people to himself at a mountain top. All the controversy with Pharaoh was about letting the Hebrew people go worship God at Mount Sinai.

And who, exactly, is at the foot of the mountain (Exodus 19:1–2)? It is thought that the whole congregation was around a million souls, counting women and children, of all the twelve tribes of Israel. Their Exodus had drawn them out of Egypt under Moses. Remember Moses's name means "drawn out." God drew them all out of Egypt to himself on the mountain, and thereafter Moses was considered the great prophet of the Old Testament whom the Messiah would follow (Deuteronomy 18:18).

Suddenly they were a nation. A nation which God was about to call into covenant with him. Beloved, God is always drawing us to himself in order to give himself to us in covenant, but sometimes we are so full of Egypt that we don't even know it.

Before God gives himself to the people, he conducts a review of sorts. He reminds the people of all he has already done on their behalf. If they covenanted with him, if they obeyed him and kept the covenant, God promised to make them his special treasure (Exodus 19:3–6). He would lavish special attention on them and make them a kingdom of priests and a holy nation. Israel would become entirely unique from every other nation in existence at that time and forevermore, because of its relationship with the living God. All the other nations would learn of the Lord God through them, and they would attract and lead others to correctly worship him.

The people readily agreed, and prepared to meet God on the mountain where God would speak audibly to Moses so the whole nation would know God was present. In anticipation of meeting God, they were required to make special purity preparations. And then...

On the morning of the third day, there were thunders and lightnings, and a thick cloud upon the mountain, and a very loud trumpet blast, so that all the people who were in the camp trembled. Then Moses brought the people out of the camp to meet God; and they took their stand at the foot of the mountain. And Mount Sinai was wrapped in smoke, because the Lord descended upon it in fire; and the smoke of it went up like the smoke of a kiln, and the whole mountain quaked greatly. And as the sound of the trumpet grew louder and louder, Moses spoke, and God answered him in thunder. And the Lord came down upon Mount Sinai, to the top of the mountain; and the Lord called Moses to the top of the mountain, and Moses went up. (Exodus 19:16–20)

Read it again, very slowly. Pretend you are there. Can you imagine being present for this? The dark mountain of Sinai was the center of storm and seismic activity.

I'm not sure why tears spring to my eyes, except that I (Sonja) want to be there, screwing my eyes tightly shut the whole time, praying I'm not annihilated by the glorious tornado of unbearable, thundering holiness whirling violently around that mountain. Hallelujah! Although in imagining this event, we certainly understand the terror of the people of Israel; they knew from the patriarchs that no one could look upon God's face and live. But we cannot say we share their ultimate desire, as they refused to come near God again for fear (Exodus 20:18–21).

Yet here the Almighty, the King of the ages, coming to commune with them. They trembled in one accord, saying, "Let me not hear again the voice of the Lord my God. Don't let me see this great fire anymore lest I die."

Never was the nation so unified in their desire. Never was a nation so fearful. The fear of the Lord abounded in every heart. Every person knew that he or she was unclean before the Almighty, so they spoke as one, asking that Moses be their intercessor—their go-between, their mediator. Whatever God had for them could be given to Moses, who in turn would tell the people God's message as he had done before in the events leading up to their redemption.

Moses became the mediator of the people throughout their journey through the Promised Land. But you have no idea how fervently Deacon Harold and I pray you are not one of those timid Israelites, drawing back from God for the fear of his presence.

When I (Sonja) was about eight, I read *The Lion, the Witch, and the Wardrobe* by C.S. Lewis. Because I was so young, I did not remember very much about the story, but what I did remember stayed with me, mysteriously, all the way into adulthood. When I saw the movie a few years ago, I was startled by a quote that I remembered. It was one sentence: "Of course he isn't safe. But he is good!"

How true that sentiment is. God's power is so matchless it *is* terrifying. But he's good. Oh, how we want you to be a Moses to those around you. We want you to be the one standing inside the thundering, lightning, pounding, quaking, dark fire, hearing the voice of God like a trumpet in your heart! Amen?

CALLED FOR WORSHIP/COMMUNION

At the top of that mountain—the mountain of God, Sinai—with the people at its base, Moses received the formal covenant. It spans the next twelve chapters of Exodus and includes the Ten Commandments and the instructions for the tabernacle of worship.

In Exodus 31:18, we read that God gave Moses as a "keepsake" for the people, the gift of the Ten Commandments on stone tablets, written by the "finger of God." Deacon Harold and I find that to be a very tender thought. We also find this type of intimate terminology for the written Word of God in the New Testament. In 2 Timothy 3:16, we read that "all Scripture is *inspired* by God" (emphasis added). *Inspired* means "God-breathed."

With "breath and finger," God wrote you a keepsake, a love letter of sorts, an invitation to risk everything with him. The Bible is the epic story of how determined God is to draw us to himself and give himself to us. By recording it all in writing, we can know when we are worshipping in a way that places us in the closest possible proximity to him. "All Scripture is inspired by God and profitable for teaching, for reproof, for correction, and for training in *righteousness*" (2 Timothy 3:16, emphasis added). Very simply, this word means "what is right."

From the foot of Mount Sinai, Moses was called to lead a nation to right-worship. At that very same mountain, Moses received the Ten Words and the whole Mosaic Law (the Torah or Pentateuch) through which he would instruct the people in proper worship through the tabernacle that would be built at its base. "The 'ten words'...belong to God's revelation of himself and his glory. The gift of the Commandments is the gift of God himself and his holy will. In making his will known, God reveals himself to his people. The gift of the commandments and of the Law is part of the covenant God sealed with his own" (*CCC*, 2059–2060).

Moses placed himself at God's disposal and was faithful. The new nation of God made it to the mountain to which God had called them from the beginning. They were about do at the foot of it what he desired all along: worship. The nation would remember this event forever.

A House for God

I (Sonja) have never built a house from the ground up. We live in an old farmhouse that we have been working on and remodeling for years. But I have heard that if you want a divorce, you should build a house. Luckily, the experience of tabernacle building was not that way for the Israelites.

God led his people out of bondage to meet and worship with him on Mount Sinai. It was a terrifying experience, and one they never forgot as a people. The rest of the book of Exodus is the account of what occurred on Mount Sinai and the instructions Moses was given. The instructions include the laws and Ten Commandments, a liturgical worship schedule, worship procedures, and the elaborate, detailed instructions for the tabernacle and furnishings. Skilled workmen carried out the important task of building and making everything. The tabernacle structure is what we are going to look at next, because it was the center of the "how" of the Old Testament.

After leading his Old Testament people out of Egyptian slavery, God told them, through Moses, that he desired to live with them. Think about that for a moment. The same God who created solar systems, DNA, and seahorses, wants to live and remain close to you. The word tabernacle literally means *to dwell*. In the instructions God gave to Moses on Mount Sinai were detailed plans for a physical worship structure that would be his new "home" in the midst of his people.

> Speak to the people of Israel, that they take for me an offering; from every man whose heart makes him willing, you shall receive the offering for me.... And let them make me a sanctuary, that I may dwell in their midst. According to all that I show you concerning the pattern of the tabernacle, and of all its furniture, so you shall make it. (Exodus 25:2, 8–9)

God wanted his new home to be made from offerings given to him by his people. Whatever gifts they might give for the purpose, God would show them exactly how to use them to make his new tabernacle. As a Catholic, the term *tabernacle* probably makes you think of the place in your church that houses the ciborium containing the Blessed Sacrament. But we'd like you to think of the tabernacle in several other distinct ways.

OLD TESTAMENT TABERNACLE

The first is the Old Testament tabernacle. Throughout history, the tabernacle was the outward sign and reminder of God's desire to be surrounded by his people, to be present with and to live among them as the heartbeat of their existence.

It was a tent, of sorts, and the portable place of worship for the nomadic Israelites who lived directly outside its gates. Their camp-sites surrounded the tabernacle by tribe on all sides in a picture of perfect design and order in what seemed like chaotic wandering in the wilderness. God placed each Israelite tribe in a specific position facing the tabernacle (Numbers 2). The camp was divided into four sets of three tribes at each compass point with one flag for each tribe.

Because one's identity was derived from his tribe and also his position in relation to the tabernacle, the tribal organization offered security to the Israelites in their relationship to the living God who dwelt there. Sometimes in the Scriptures the term tabernacle indicates the whole temple area. Other times it refers to the tent sanctuary itself. This was the layout of the sanctuary:

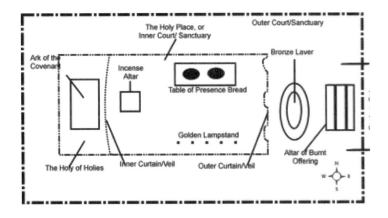

The Courtyard

Located in the outer courtyard, just inside the gate, was a BBQ-grill-like structure for ritual burnt offerings. Large enough to burn up an entire heifer, the fire for this altar fell from heaven as from the presence of God from the first sacrificial offering and was never to go out. Remember that the livelihood of the people was intimately tied to their livestock. The daily animal sacrifices offered on the altar were a constant reminder that sin causes death and that atonement is the first requirement for entering into the presence of God.

The next worship element was the bronze laver full of water, an oversized birdbath-shaped structure used for washing the blood and dirt off the priests' hands and feet before they entered the enclosed sanctuary for their ministry duties (Exodus 30:18–20, 40:30–32). The constant washing taught the people that after atonement for sin, purity was necessary to draw near to God in the sanctuary.

The Sanctuary

Outside in the courtyard of the tabernacle, everything was about blood, judgment, death, cleansing, and purification. But in the sanctuary of the Holy Place, everything was about life, nourishment, light, and the fragrance of incense. In here, it was quiet, silent even.

If you think about it, our own churches illustrate this principle. Outside the church, in the world, is where all our weekly personal offerings and sacrifices and work occur. Then we enter the narthex, where our boisterous chatter, laughter, and fellowship takes place.

However, once we enter the holy space, the sanctuary, all is still and quiet. The red sanctuary lamp flickers there, inviting us into its womb of prayer.

Just inside the thick outer curtain protecting the sanctuary of the tabernacle, it was cool and dim. Incense hung in the air as the priest went about his duties in the glow of the man-sized golden menorah to his immediate left.

The gold table of presence bread was located to the right, opposite the lampstand, while the incense altar stood straight ahead in front of another thick, embroidered curtain. The priest was responsible for keeping the seven oil lamps of the menorah full of oil and their wicks trimmed at all times. The twelve loaves of presence bread, also called bread of the face (of God), represented the twelve tribes of Israel, and the priest kept the bread fresh and replenished on a weekly basis. The bread was called presence bread because it was placed in the presence of God, and God was present in it, in the tabernacle.

The incense altar was a smaller version of the outdoor sacrificial altar on which a special recipe of incense burned perpetually. Altogether these elements of sanctuary furniture communicated that light, sustenance, and prayer are in the presence of God.

The Inner Sanctuary, the Holy of Holies

Just inside the inner curtain separating the Holy Place from the Holy of Holies was the ark, the most sacred of all the furniture in the tabernacle, because it was here on which the presence of God rested in the pillar of fire and cloud. Inside the ark, the Hebrews kept a copy of the Ten Commandments to summarize and symbolize the unsurpassed gift of the whole Law, a memorial pot of the daily manna from heaven to stress God's faithful daily provision, and Aaron's budded rod to remind them they lived under the protective authority of an institutional priesthood, all of it according to the explicit instruction and will of God.

Everything in the tabernacle was specified by God himself to Moses, down to the last detail. The weight of all the gold used in the construction of the tabernacle is thought to be about a ton! The gold and silver and brass, all the jewels and linens—everything needed to construct and decorate the tabernacle and its furnishings according to God's instructions—was provided by God from their enemies and slave masters, the Egyptians. "The people of Israel had also done as

Moses told them, for they had asked of the Egyptians jewelry of silver and of gold, and clothing; and the Lord had given the people favor in the sight of the Egyptians, so that they let them have what they asked. Thus they despoiled the Egyptians" (Exodus 12:35–36). Friend, whatever you have suffered can also be turned into the treasure that will furnish and decorate the sanctuary of your heart.

Although it was a tent and portable, the Old Testament tabernacle was not a substitute dwelling, but a glorious shrine that symbolized the presence of God living in the midst of his people. The tabernacle was the "how" of the Old Testament people, the locus of their communal life and worship. All the seasons and liturgical festivals of the year centered around it, especially the sacred family meal of Passover when the Passover lamb was offered on the altar of burnt offering every spring.

Perhaps most importantly, the tabernacle was a copy of the sanctuary in heaven and the prototype of the Church to come: "They serve a copy and shadow of the heavenly sanctuary" (Hebrews 8:5). The reason God specified the tabernacle, its liturgical worship, and its elements in such great detail to Moses in the Law at Mount Sinai is because it was patterned after the one in heaven.

In the Bible, we see that God desires a particular kind of worship. That means worship is not about me, what I like, or whether I am being entertained or satisfied by what is happening. Deacon Harold likes to say if you're not being fed at Mass, it's because you're accustomed to junk food, and you don't get junk food at Mass. There is a place for all of that in the Church, but it's not in worship. Worship is about God, what he wants, what glorifies and reveals him most, and what draws us into the closest possible proximity to him in heaven. For these reasons, God also specified in great detail how the tabernacle should be built, filled, and used.

Proper worship was meant to include liturgy, ritual, and ceremony. The Old Testament tabernacle included a priesthood, an altar, altar fire, a water basin, a light source, bread and wine, incense, a special curtain, a throne for God, a liturgy, and a liturgical schedule. Each of these things was required for proper worship, according to God and specified by him. In addition, each element was required to remain, perpetually, throughout the generations of his people (cf. Exodus 25—31). In, with, and through Christ, they do.

THE CLOUD AND THE GLORY

After Moses faithfully supervised the people's obedience to God's instructions regarding building and assembling the tabernacle, something astonishing happened: "Then the cloud covered the tent of meeting, and the glory of the Lord filled the tabernacle. And Moses was not able to enter the tent of meeting, because the cloud rested upon it, and the glory of the Lord filled the tabernacle" (Exodus 40:34–35). Glory! Literally!

The presence of God was literal, and the people saw it in the pillar of cloud resting on the throne from within the tabernacle. They called this cloud the "*Shekinah*" glory. *Shekinah* means "to dwell." The presence of God was literal, and the people saw it in the pillar of cloud resting on the tabernacle.

Can you imagine what it would have been like to *see* something of the unseeable God—this miraculous accommodation of his glorious presence for his people to witness? How do you think the people felt?

God was really present in the miraculous pillar of cloud and fire, leading his people (Exodus 40:36–38). And he still is. Sort of. Next, we'll look at the "how" of the New Testament.

LET'S REVIEW

This is how God's people worshipped in the Old Testament, his scriptural blueprint for your life.

- *God is always calling us* to worship in his presence.
- *God explains how to worship* him properly.
- *God wants to make a home in us.*

- *Moses was the Great Prophet* of the Old Testament.
- *Through Moses's mediation, God saved his people* through the exodus from Egypt, provided manna for their nourishment, and taught the people his Law.
- *In the Old Testament Law, God detailed instructions* for an institutional priesthood and liturgical worship centered around the tabernacle, including an annual, sacred family Passover meal with a Passover lamb.
- *The tabernacle included a table of presence bread* and a memorial pot of manna from heaven.
- *The Old Testament tabernacle was a copy of the sanctuary in heaven* and the prototype of the Church to come.

INVITATION

My (Deacon Harold's) earliest memory of being a tabernacle of God was through prayer as a small child. Every night, I knelt at the side of my bed and repeated the words of my mother: "Our Father, who art in heaven... Hail Mary, full of grace... Lovely Lady dressed in blue, teach me how to pray..." My mother was my first and deepest spiritual influence. She made every effort to instill the love and truth of the Lord Jesus Christ into my heart by her words and, more importantly, by her example of untiring self-sacrifice and total self-giving. In my eyes, my mother epitomized Christian humility and faith, and it was from her that I developed a deep love for the Mass and fostered a devotion to the Blessed Mother.

When I reached the fourth grade, my mother encouraged me to become an altar boy, which I did with much enthusiasm and great fervor. It was a responsibility that I took very seriously, so much so that people used to comment on how serious I looked on the altar and noticed that I never smiled. I always felt honored when I was chosen to serve at special functions where the Archbishop was present.

During this time, I was also active in faith discussion groups, joined the parish choir, and attended youth retreats. It was as an altar boy, however, where I developed a profound respect for the priesthood.

I remember the moment like it was yesterday. I was serving Sunday Mass as a twelve-year-old and was just about to ring the bells during the elevation of the Eucharist and thought, *I could do what the priest is doing.* I had always loved being at the altar and believed that God might be calling me to the priesthood. During the sacrifice of the Mass, I felt closest to Christ and experienced the power of his love in an intensely personal way. The mystery and beauty of the Mass enamored me, and my love for Jesus deepened with each passing year.

God Prompt—LOVE the Word

Lectio—Listen

Then the cloud covered the tent of meeting, and the glory of the Lord filled the tabernacle. And Moses was not able to enter the tent of meeting, because the cloud abode upon it, and the glory of the Lord filled the tabernacle. Throughout all their journeys, whenever the cloud was taken up from over the tabernacle, the people of Israel would go onward; but if the cloud was not taken up, then they did not go onward till the day that it was taken up. For throughout all their journeys the cloud of the Lord was upon the tabernacle by day, and fire was in it by night, in the sight of all the house of Israel. (Exodus 40:34–38)

Oratio—Observe

Imagine the celebration as the tabernacle you helped construct with your own offerings is finally finished. Are there tambourines? Dancing? Are the children frolicking, as wild with excitement as their parents? What did you offer? Gold, linen, balsams for the anointing oil or incense, your services as craftsman, embroiderer, or goldsmith?

Are the people all gathered around, or are you gazing at the incredible sight from the flap of your own tent?

Does the sky grow dark when the unworldly cloud descends and engulfs the tabernacle? Is the air charged with shock or fear or thrill? What does it sound like as it falls, or maybe it simply appears? Are you afraid? Excited? Awed? Are you surprised as darkness approaches that the cloud changes to fire? That you can see it no matter where you are in the whole camp, even from the back side of Sinai?

Does the presence of that cloud comfort you when you look at it in the days to come, knowing he's there somehow, leading you through this barren desert, day and night, every second?

Meditatio—Verbalize

What an incredible, glorious thought: that you are with me, Lord, leading me and guiding me every moment, and that you are building a sanctuary in me with my very own offerings. I want to offer everything! But I confess a tremor of fear when I think of your presence in the tabernacle of my body, because I have not made it as hospitable as it could be for you, and my offerings have not been generous. I need to know that you love me unconditionally, even though the tabernacle of my body and heart is not always pure enough to welcome you. What can I offer you, today, as a welcome present?

Contemplatio—Entrust

Perhaps you'd like to wonder at and cherish, now, your promise of his unfailing presence with you.

chapter seven

The How of the New Testament

As a former denominational non-Catholic (Sonja), our worship structure looked like this: welcome and announcements, uplifting congregational hymn, pastoral prayer, congregational hymn, offering, choir special or other special music, sermon, invitation, and benediction. Altogether, the worship service consisted of about fifteen minutes of singing hymns, and a forty-five-minute teaching sermon. Every non-Catholic worship service I ever participated in followed this tradition, or liturgy.

The more I learned in the Bible about Old Testament tabernacle worship, however, the more I wondered why God would specify Old Testament tabernacle worship so carefully and hold his people to it so strictly throughout their generations if New Testament worship wasn't supposed to be anything like it, and heavenly worship in Revelation was *nothing* like it. Although I enjoyed and learned from it immensely, I couldn't find my worship service in the Bible at all, except where St. Paul's preaching was so long-winded that Eutychus finally drifted to sleep after midnight and fell out a window (Acts 20:9). If Old Testament worship was preparation for New Testament and heavenly worship, shouldn't they be similar and recognizable? So it was, partly, the connections between the Old Testament tabernacle and Catholic liturgy and worship that drew me into Catholicism.

As the "how" of the Old Testament centered around the tabernacle, so does the New, but with the cleverest of twists that only God could think up.

THE NEW TABERNACLE

In Luke 1, the human race receives the stunning news for the first time. "And the angel said to her, 'Do not be afraid, Mary, for you have found favor with God. And behold, you will conceive in your womb and bear a son, and you shall call his name Jesus.... Therefore the child to be born will be called holy, the Son of God'" (Luke 1:30–35). A human being will be a tabernacle for God.

I have always found this account fascinating, partly because God tells Mary how pleased he is with her, and I long to hear those words from him myself. And then there's the God of the cosmos getting himself all dirty and stuff by being one of us. But I am also captivated by Mary's reaction.

Although she was not as terrified as the Israelites at the foot of Mount Sinai, Mary appears somewhat disturbed by the whole episode, "And Mary said to the angel, 'How shall this be, since I have no husband?'" (Luke 1:34). Have you ever experienced God in a way that disturbed you?

At the Annunciation, the Virgin Mary is told the power of the Holy Spirit will "come upon," or "overshadow" her. That almost gives me the shivers. In the Greek version of the Old Testament (Septuagint), sometimes called the apostles' Scriptures, the language is exactly the same as that in Exodus 40:34–35: "Then the cloud covered the tent of meeting, and the glory of the Lord filled the tabernacle. And Moses was not able to enter the tent of meeting, because the cloud *abode upon* it, and the glory of the Lord filled the tabernacle" (emphasis added).

Viewing Luke 1:35 and Exodus 40:34–35 together reveals that the presence of God rested upon Mary in a way similar to God's presence in the tabernacle. This was the moment when the new covenant was conceived within Mary, who is called the Ark of the New Covenant by the Church Fathers. Glorious. Marvelous. Miraculous. Breathless.

Just as the Old Testament physical worship structure was the first manifestation of the tabernacle, Mary and Jesus are two other manifestations of the tabernacle. This shocking, glorious presence through Christ with men is why we bow deeply at the words "was incarnate of the Virgin Mary and became man" in the Creed during the Mass. In Jesus the tabernacle, God dwelt again with man, and the special glory of the Lord rested on him, just as it did on and in Mary, his mother, and once had in the pillar of cloud in the Old Testament tabernacle.

For this reason, she is also given the title *Theotokos* by the Church, meaning "mother of God." And it is at this moment that Mary becomes the very first living tabernacle. She is the living temple in whom the Son of God, the second person of the Trinity, made human nature the house in which he dwells. The tabernacle of his flesh was formed wholly from hers (see Genesis 3:15).

God was really present in the Old Testament tabernacle, in the pillar of cloud and fire, leading his people. He was literally present in Mary at the Incarnation. The first thing she and Joseph do with the new baby, as obedient Jewish parents of God, is to present Jesus in the temple according to Jewish law. There, they ascended the temple stones in Jerusalem, summing up the Old Testament and ushering in something wonderfully new—something similar to the old, but fresh, vibrant, and mercifully new.

Thousands of years after the original Old Testament occupation of the cloud and fire in the tabernacle, the Gospel of John applies a particularly special designation to the new way God was present with man in Christ. The cloud and fire, the *Shekinah* glory, came to dwell with us again in an especially tender, miraculous, and surprising way. "And the Word became flesh and dwelt among us, and we beheld his glory" (John 1:14). "Dwelt" in this context literally means "tabernacled," while *Shekinah* means "glory." Jesus is the new tabernacle where the glory of God dwells.

This glory-presence foreshadowed Eucharistic Adoration and benediction today. As the incense rises before the Lord—in the presence of the people, singing *O Salutaris* and *Tantum Ergo*—the God of the Universe is with his sons and daughters in the monstrance (from the Latin word *monstrare*, meaning "to show"). The flesh for the life of the world, Jesus Christ, shows us his "face," and is truly and substantially present—body, blood, soul, and divinity—in the most Blessed Sacrament of the altar.

Jesus connected his body to the new temple, himself: "Destroy this temple and in three days I will raise it up" (John 2:19). Wrote Cardinal Joseph Ratzinger, "This is a prophecy of the Cross: he shows that the destruction of his earthly body will be at the same time the end of the [Old Testament Jewish] Temple. With his resurrection the new Temple will begin: the living body of Jesus Christ, which will now stand in the sight of God and be the place of all worship. Into this body he incorporates men. It is the tabernacle that no human hands have made, the place of true worship of God, which casts out the shadow and replaces it with reality."[1]

In a very real sense, everything true of the Old Testament tabernacle is also true of us, individually and as the Church, because we are tabernacles too. "Christ is the true tabernacle of God, 'the place where his glory dwells'; by the grace of God, Christians also become the temples of the Holy Spirit, living stones out of which the Church is built" (*CCC*, 1197). Through us, the Church, God is literally present, living on the earth as the soul of the world.[2]

In the Old Testament, God dwelt in a portable tent, and it was the center of communal life for his people and the place of worship. The tabernacle was patterned after the one in heaven, and it foreshadowed the Church to come.

In the New Testament, God dwells in a living tabernacle, the body of Christ, the Church, made of living stones (1 Peter 2:5). We *are* the church! When we gather together in our own churches to worship, God is present in and through us all. "In its earthly state the Church needs places where the community can gather together. Our visible churches, holy places, are images of the holy city, the heavenly Jerusalem, toward which we are making our way on pilgrimage" (*CCC,* 1198). So what is Christian worship, the "how" of the New Testament? Just like the new temple, the "how" of the New Testament is built on the foundation of the Old.

THE NEW MOSES

They didn't intend to start a new religion. They had made a discovery. As far as they were concerned, it was the discovery of a lifetime—many, many lifetimes, in fact—and they were excited. The way they explained it showed their thrilled understanding that the millennia of waiting were finished for the Jews; their quest was over; the promise was here: The Messiah had finally come.

The first thing Andrew did was find his brother Simon: "'We have found the Messiah' (which means Christ)" (John 1:41). Philip also told his brother Nathaniel, "We have found him of whom Moses in the Law and also the Prophets wrote—Jesus of Nazareth, son of Joseph" (John 1:45).

What were these two Jewish men talking about? What is this Messiah of whom Moses and the prophets spoke?

Just before the children of Israel entered the Promised Land, God conducted a review of sorts, a summary of the Law, that is recorded for us in the book of Deuteronomy (meaning "second law"). Tucked in the middle, in the eighteenth chapter, Moses offered a remarkable prophecy. In recalling the national experience that was memorialized and burned into their consciousness, the text describes how the coming prophet would be like Moses, the great Old Testament prophet.

"I will raise up for them a prophet like you from among their brethren; and I will put my words in his mouth, and he shall speak to them all that I command him. And whoever will not give heed to my words which he shall speak in my name, I myself will require it of him" (Deuteronomy 18:18–19).

One day a new Moses would speak for God to the people, and everything that mediator would speak or require would be God's word and God's requirement. God's word and will would be transmitted through that very special mediator. So the primary way that the new prophet was to be "like Moses" was in the role of go-between or mediator.

In Bible days, every priest, prophet, and king was an intermediary or intercessor who represented God on behalf of the people. The priest offered prayers and sacrifices and stood in the Holy Place on behalf of the people. The prophets were also intercessors who mediated God's word and often called the nation to repentance from sin and to return to covenant relationship with him.

Kings like David and Solomon were also like Moses in that they led and administered the Law to the whole nation. Because a king is a judge in peace and a commander in war, Israel's kings acted in God's stead to mediate God's will and were intercessors acting on God's behalf.

Prophets, priests, and kings were all anointed to show and facilitate their consecration. Moses, in a sense, fulfilled all three functions of the old covenant mediator at the same time. Peter's sermon in Acts 3:22 quotes Moses's prophecy and makes it clear that it speaks of Christ. Moses was a *type* of the Messiah to come.

In Scripture, a *type* is a person, thing, action, or event that precedes and foreshadows a new, greater person, thing, action or event.[3] That which is prefigured is referred to as an *antitype*. To be a true antitype, it must be in all ways better than the type that came before it. Types are usually found in the Old Testament; they bear similarity but are always inferior to their antitypes. Antitypes are usually found in the New Testament as the fulfillment of what prefigured them. Types have their own unique historical importance and reality, but they were intended by the Holy Spirit to also prefigure something greater to come.

For example, the new covenant is the antitype of the old covenant type, and is in all ways better than the old (Hebrews 8:13). Moses was the great Old Testament prophet, a true historical person of God, a type, who prefigured Christ, the antitype.

The word *Messiah* means "anointed." Just as Old Testament prophets, priests, and kings were anointed with oil to consecrate them for service, Jesus, the New Moses, was specially anointed by the Holy Spirit, which the oil prefigured, to mediate the new covenant in his very person. Like Moses, Jesus died, but as the superior antitype, he rose from the dead to carry on a better ministry forever (Acts 3:15). In Jesus, we have a new covenant, a new priesthood, a new sacrifice, a new Passover, a new law, a new liturgy, and a new manna. Indeed, Jesus makes all things new (Revelation 21:5).

A NEW SACRIFICE

For all of the things that are praiseworthy about Moses's life, one episode is often overlooked: "Now it came to pass on the next day that Moses said to the people, 'You have committed a great sin. So now I will go up to the Lord; perhaps I can make atonement for your sin.' Then Moses returned to the Lord and said, 'Oh, these people have committed a great sin, and have made for themselves a god of gold! Yet now, if you will forgive their sin—but if not, I pray, blot me out of your book which you have written.' And the Lord said to Moses, 'Whoever has sinned against me, I will blot him out of my book" (Exodus 32:30–33).

The prophet to come, the Messiah, would most resemble Moses in offering himself to die for the sins of the people. In order that Israel might be saved from the wrath of God, Moses stood ready to offer his own life—to take the punishment of the people's sins on himself if God could find no other way to forgive them. He asked God that his life be an expiation, or satisfaction, for the sins of the people. As a priest he could have made grandiose offerings—thousands of lambs or bulls—but instead he simply offered his own life.

Remember that forty years of Moses's life were spent as a shepherd in the mountains and deserts of Midian. In leading the people, he showed the mindset and attitudes of a good shepherd.

The job description of a good shepherd calls for the kind of serious commitment in which one must be willing to give his own life for the sheep, as Jesus explained most succinctly in John: "I am the good shepherd. The good shepherd gives his life for the sheep" (John 10:11).

Moses was willing to die for God's people, but as a sinner himself he could not atone for the peoples' sin. He could only prepare for the Messiah by instituting the temporary sacrifices of the Passover lamb and the daily animal sacrifices of the tabernacle that foreshadowed him.

Jesus, both priest and victim, the spotless "Lamb who takes away the sins of the world" (John 1:29), offers himself as the sacrifice. He is the Good Shepherd who lays down his life for the sheep. In so doing, he has the full authority of God himself: "And whoever will not give heed to my words which he shall speak in my name, I myself will require it of him" (Deuteronomy 18:18–19).

A New Law

The Letter to the Hebrews tells us that a new law was necessary because while the Old Testament Law laid out what was true, right, and good, it could not bring its commandments to "perfection," meaning there was no power or grace in it to bring about the good that it commanded (Hebrews 7:11,19). In essence, God gave his people the old covenant to teach them, remember, how to worship properly. The Law was mostly concerned with their outward behaviors, and it was a guardian (cf. Galatians 3:19–25) for the people until the Messiah could come with real depth and power.

Indeed, when the fullness of time was come, God was faithful to send the Son and begin working in their inward motivations as well as their outward behaviors, and this Son would bring with him and impart the grace and power necessary to live more deeply, more fully, more purely in a way that reached the perfection of holiness.

From the first burst of God's Word that created every photon, atom, and molecule of matter and millisecond of time, to the Incarnation that brought his Word to bear on our darkness of soul, the Holy Spirit has been at work through Jesus, miraculously creating, ordering, illuminating, generating—*igniting*.

Hidden no more, from the opening lines of the gospels Jesus walks into our history, our world, and our lives as no other ever has. Jesus brings God to us. Jesus is among us. And like the first Law from Mount Sinai of old, Jesus begins with a Sermon on the Mount.

THE BEATITUDES

St. Teresa of Calcutta once spoke on the relationship between holiness and sacrifice, saying, "For a sacrifice to be real, it must cost, must hurt, must make us empty ourselves. Give yourself fully to God. He will use you to accomplish great things on the condition that you believe much more in his love than in your own weakness."

In the Sermon on the Mount, Jesus challenges humanity to go deeper than the letter of the Old Testament Law to the spirit under it, to a deeper, life-giving love like our Heavenly Father's love. The key to understanding the blessings of the Beatitudes (*blessed* means "bliss") is acknowledging and affirming our total dependence on God's love.

In saying "yes" to Christ's invitation to live with him in the Father and the Holy Spirit, who fills us with the fire of God's love and ignites the flame of our love in return, we live the Beatitudes in response to God's divine life in us!

Blessed are the poor in spirit. The poor in spirit acknowledge their spiritual poverty and human frailty and know how much they need the help and support of God.

Blessed are those who mourn. Those who grieve in sorrow are assured of comfort and consolation from a loving, faith-filled community that forms the Body of Christ. Our Blessed Mother possesses a genuinely feminine heart of love and is the perfect example of what it means to be fully human. In her sorrowful heart we find true solace, comfort, and peace.

Blessed are the meek. Meekness is power under control. The meek reach out to care for others in compassion and tenderness, not force or manipulation. They sacrifice their own needs in confidence and deliberation out of a constant awareness of the needs of others. "We think sometimes that poverty is only being hungry, naked and homeless. The poverty of being unwanted, unloved, and uncared for is the greatest poverty" (St. Teresa of Calcutta).

Blessed are those who hunger and thirst for righteousness. These saints work to ensure that wrongs are righted wherever they appear. Everyone receives the opportunity to live a life of dignity and self-respect. Today, police officers, firefighters, and soldiers know that the greatest gift they can give is to lay their life on the line—and to even sacrifice that life—so that others may live.

Blessed are the merciful. Understanding that "mercy triumphs over judgment" (James 2:13), the merciful extend compassion and forgiveness. St. Louis IX, the French king who was a great lover of justice, was renowned for his charity. He washed the feet of the poor, ministered to lepers, and provided food for over one hundred people throughout his kingdom daily. Imagine what kind of world it would be if our political leaders followed his example!

Blessed are the pure in heart. These saints see God's presence in every person and experience without prejudice or bias. They see others the way God sees them. As Mother Teresa so beautifully reminds us: "Let us touch the dying, the poor, the lonely and the unwanted according to the graces we have received, and let us not be ashamed or slow to do God's humble work."

Blessed are the peacemakers. Rebellion and division were the sin of Satan and are his work. Peacemakers work for unity without sacrificing righteousness or mercy.

Blessed are those who are persecuted for righteousness sake. Blessed indeed are those who have the fortitude and strength to put the values of truth, love, and justice for all above their own survival.

Blessed are you when men revile you and persecute you and utter all kinds of evil against you falsely on my account. We are called to preach the Gospel in its fullness and not just the parts that we like! This means that when we live our faith every day through the witness of our lives—when we defend the right to life for all human beings from the moment of conception until natural death, when we defend the dignity of marriage and family life—we will be persecuted, mocked, ridiculed, and scorned just as Christ was as he made his way to Calvary.

Life is too short for us to worry about what other people think. We are called by God to be saints: to live our faith with courage and conviction in this time and in this place, and to put all our trust in God. As the Scriptures encourage us, "For God alone my sold waits in silence, / for my hope is from him. / He only is my rock and my salvation, / my fortress; I shall not be shaken" (Psalm 62:6–7). We are to rejoice and be glad, for our reward will be great in heaven!

The Beatitudes form a foundation for holiness and make clear what is expected of a follower of Jesus. All of the beatitudes point to our participation in the kingdom of heaven here on earth: a society that exists according to these values of truth and love, of compassion and mercy, of peace and freedom—all qualities which flow from the very heart of God himself.

Jesus challenged dry rule-keepers to respond generously to the love of God showered on them. Because he plunges beneath its surface, all of the old law is included in the new. Nothing is lost.

> Think not that I have come to abolish the law and the prophets; I have come not to abolish them but to fulfil them. For truly, I say to you, till heaven and earth pass away, not an iota, not a dot, will pass from the law until all is accomplished. Whoever then relaxes one of the least of these commandments and teaches men so, shall be called least in the kingdom of heaven; but he who does them and teaches them shall be called great in the kingdom of heaven. (Matthew 5:17–19)

Indeed, the Law is fulfilled so completely that it exceeds its Jewish teachers. *Word, promise,* and *commandment* are all interchangeable terms in the Scriptures. So that Jesus doesn't just hand over the Word of God in Ten Commandments to the people like Moses, Jesus *is* the Word of Law in his person (John 1:1). He is prophet, priest, and King of the new law of love (Romans 13:10; Galatians 5:14; James 2:8).

At this point, it is helpful to note that Church history makes several major distinctions in Old Testament Law: natural and moral law, ceremonial law, and civil law. In the Bible, natural and moral law is first summarized in the Ten Commandments as preparation for the Gospel. Said to be written on the human heart (Romans 2:14–15), it therefore universally applies to every person and proceeds from the unchanging eternal Law in God's mind, so it is unchangeable and unmovable by different historical times or cultures. Jesus's Sermon on the Mount is a more thorough revelation of natural and moral law involving all of creation and the entire human person: behavior and motives; exterior and interior; body, mind, and soul. This sermon functions as a summary of the whole Gospel (*CCC*, 1949–1974).

Ceremonial law regulates liturgy and worship and is the body of sacred signs that signifies spiritual realties. Liturgical laws commemorate the decisive event of salvation, the Exodus and Passover being that of the Old Testament. As Deacon Harold regularly says, the book of Leviticus can largely be described as the Jewish worship manual for this ceremonial law. Old Testament religious law communicated no grace and was therefore entirely symbolic. As the spiritual realties that the law symbolized changed with the New Testament, it was necessary that religious ceremonial laws did too.

For instance, Christians do not kill and quarter sheep and goats, haul the carcasses to the local church altar, pour their blood out at the altar's base, and burn them there as a sacrifice. But we do have a sacrificial Lamb who offers his own wholly consumed Body, Blood, soul, and divinity on the altar at every Mass just as he does continually in heaven (Revelation 5:6). The cross and resurrection of Christ is the decisive New Testament salvation event, so the Mass has been New Testament liturgical law since the apostles. Old Testament ceremonial law existed for Jesus and had to change in order to show that a new spiritual reality had come into being through his person.

Judicial precepts are circumstantial civil rules pertaining particularly to Old Testament places and history. These necessarily changed with the dawning of the New Testament. The adulterous woman is one example in which Jewish civil law required her to be stoned for adultery (outward behavior), but Jesus required that we all inspect ourselves for adulterous hearts first (inward motives). Another illustration is Jewish dietary laws that were practical for separation from the Gentiles in the Old Testament to keep the faith pure until the advent of Messiah through their lineage, but that were necessarily set aside in order to spread the Gospel to all men. One can't share with someone when he is not allowed to associate with him, after all.

As the fulfillment of the Old Testament law centered in the tabernacle, Jesus is the final priest and victim, the wholly consumed sacrifice offered as the first requirement for tabernacle worship on the altar of the cross whose blood was poured out in atonement for sin. Foreshadowed by the laver, he is the living water offered to us in Baptism to cleanse us of sin.

In the sanctuary, he is the Light of the world, the antitype of the old menorah. He is the true incense of sacrificial prayer, and the mercy seat of propitiation. Jesus is the fulfillment of all Old Testament signs: "And beginning at Moses and all the Prophets, he expounded to them in all the Scriptures the things concerning himself" (Luke 24:27). Indeed, all Scripture speaks of him. "For the testimony of Jesus is the spirit of prophecy" (Revelation 19:10), as St. Irenaeus maintained:

> If anyone, therefore, reads the Scriptures with attention, he will find in them an account of Christ, and a foreshadowing of the new calling (*vocationis*). For Christ is the treasure which was hid in the field, that is, in this world (for "the field is the world"); but the treasure hid in the Scriptures is Christ, since he was pointed out by means of types and parables. Hence his human nature could not be understood, prior to the consummation of those things which had been predicted, that is, the advent of Christ.... And the disciple will be perfected, and [rendered] like the householder, "who bringeth forth from his treasure things new and old."[4]

Indeed, perhaps the most nourishing of the old tabernacle antitypes in the "how" of the New Testament is bread.

OLD TESTAMENT BREAD

Few things are better than fresh-baked bread, still warm from the oven and slathered with enough butter to make it float. Don't you love it? For me (Sonja), it's one of life's simple pleasures, but more than that, bread is the basis of nourishment for every civilization and people. God included it in the tabernacle to show how, one day, it would be the basis of nourishment in the spiritual life as well, as the tabernacle presence bread was a type of our Holy Eucharist.

Presence bread was a reminder of God's perpetual provision and a communal offering. Along with the bread, there were also offerings of incense and wine at the table. Because it was located in the tabernacle, where God's presence dwelt, it was bread where God was present, and which was placed perpetually in his presence. The bread was in the tabernacle because it was holy bread; it was holy bread because it was in the presence of God in the tabernacle.

Even while the people moved through the wilderness, the "continual bread" was to remain on the gold table (Numbers 4:5–7), and like the other tabernacle elements, the presence bread observance was to last forever (Leviticus. 24:5–9). Throughout their history, God taught the Israelites the particular significance of bread offerings in several important ways.

According to the Church Fathers, the best way to determine how the Scriptures intend a word, idea, or element (like bread) to be understood is by looking at the first Biblical occurrence. The first offering of bread and wine to God occurs at the hands of Melchizedek in Genesis 14:18–20.

Melchizedek's biblical entrance and exit (or lack thereof) both occur in these three verses in Genesis 14:18–20: "And Mel-chiz'edek king of Salem brought out bread and wine; he was priest of God Most High. And he blessed him and said, 'Blessed be Abram by God Most High, maker of heaven and earth; and blessed be God Most

High, who has delivered your enemies into your hand!' And Abram gave him a tenth of everything" (Genesis 14:18–20).

Melchizedek just appears in the Scriptures out of nowhere in the middle of a conflict between Abram and another king. Despite the three-verse brevity of his description in Genesis, many other biblical authors place enormous importance on Melchizedek. We also hear his name in the Church's first Eucharistic Prayer of the Mass: "Be pleased to look upon these offerings...and to accept them, as once you were pleased to accept the...offering of your high priest Melchizedek."

Melchizak was king of Salem, a word meaning "peace" (Genesis 14:18). Salem was an early name for what would later become Jerusalem, the capital of the Jewish people. We also see that Melchizedek was a priest of God, the very first priest mentioned in the Bible. These three verses imply it was *because* he was a priest that he offered bread and wine.

We also know that he simply appears and disappears on the biblical scene, and that somehow he was greater than Abraham, since only one who is greater can bless another or receive a tithe from him. Melchizedek was a type of Christ.

Jesus succeeds Melchizedek and is therefore greater than both Abraham and Melchizedek. For instance, in Psalm 110, a psalm (song) of King David, Jesus himself identified David as its author and interpreted it to be a psalm prophetic of the Messiah. So did Old Testament Jews and Sts. Peter, Paul, and Stephen. Psalm 110:4 says that the Messiah will be of "the order of Melchizedek," meaning "in succession" and "an established system" of. Remember that Melchizedek offered bread and wine? The bread and wine our new Melchizedek offers is rooted in the Old Testament bread in several ways.

In Exodus 12 we find the description of the Passover bread, one of the earliest offerings of bread to communicate a significant message.

Remember that Passover was instituted as a memorial, a re-participation, of that first Passover when God rescued his people from slavery to Egypt so miraculously that they did not have time for their bread to rise. They were commanded to eat the unleavened bread along with their Passover lamb, sacrificed and roasted (Exodus 13:3–10).

A little more than a month after the Israelites were rescued from Egypt that first Passover, they began to run out of food in the desert where food and water were scarce. In their weariness and probably worry, they complained against God.

"What is it?" the Israelites asked, when it appeared on the wilderness floor, and so they named it "manna," meaning "What?" (Exodus 16:14–31). Manna was heavenly bread miraculously provided by God to nourish the Israelites during the entire forty-year wilderness journey. Apparently, the manna was nutritionally balanced and complete to have nourished them for so long.

Manna appeared daily after the morning dew and melted with the sun. Small, round, "fine as frost," manna tasted like "wafers made with honey," and could be boiled, baked, or made into cakes. Manna fell every day for forty years until the people reached the Promised Land (Joshua 5:12)!

Each of these bread offerings was to be an eternal observance: Melchizedek's offering was prophetic of the Messiah; unleavened Passover bread was an everlasting annual Feast; the bread of the Presence was a perpetual staple in the tabernacle; and a memorial pot of manna was included in the ark within the Holy of Holies.

Melchizedek's offering, Passover bread, manna, and presence bread all conveyed a single theme: God was with his people forever in the most basic nourishment of life: bread. He was ever-present, carefully, lovingly feeding and providing for them. But true to type, there was another, superior reason he furnished miraculous, eternal bread in so many forms. Melchizedek's bread and wine offering, Moses's unleavened bread of the Passover, manna in the wilderness, and presence bread in the tabernacle were all types of another bread to come. The new offering and new bread is the antitype, necessarily and in all ways superior to every type that foreshadowed it.

NEW TESTAMENT BREAD

Jesus fulfills the mysterious ministry of the first priest, Melchizedek—both priests forever, kings of peace, without origin, offering bread and wine (Hebrews 5:5–6, Psalm 110:4). Jesus fulfills Moses's ministry as prophet, priest, and king, leading God's people through the final exodus to the last Promised Land as our king.

Luke 9:28–36 tells us of the transfiguration of Christ, when Jesus spoke to Moses and Elijah on Mount Tabor. Luke 9:31 says they spoke of his departure together, but the original word is *exodus*. Jesus is the new Moses on the mountain, preparing to lead his people on a new exodus from the slavery of sin and death. A new exodus needs a new manna. Jesus, the new Moses, nourishes us on God's word as prophet, and presence bread and manna as our high priest.

In John 6, Jesus offers his most personal teachings on the new manna, the Eucharist. First, Jesus illustrates how he can multiply bits of bread to feed thousands of people. Then he proves, again, that he is Lord of natural elements by walking on the sea. Once Jesus knows the people understand that he is a prophet, he compares himself to Moses, the greatest prophet in the history of God's people. Then he makes one of the boldest statements of his ministry: "I am the bread of life."

Jesus points out that his teaching here must be understood in the context of Old Testament bread. The bread of earth, of wheat and bran, and even the manna that fell from heaven, offered physical nourishment and life. But the bread that Jesus *is*, the real bread of the presence, gives life that is spiritual and eternal. Because it nourishes unto *eternal* life, it is even greater than the Old Testament bread of the presence and a true fulfillment and antitype. Once they understood how literally Jesus was speaking about eating his flesh, many disciples turned back and ceased following him (John 6:66).

In John 6, we hear Jesus teach us he is our new Melchizedek, new Moses, new manna, and new presence bread. Rather than mere bread and wine to nourish natural life, Jesus offers the bread of his body and wine of his blood for eternal life. He is our new Moses who leads and feeds us with the bread of life on our exodus to the Promised Land of heaven. He is the true presence bread, the bread of the face of God, of whom we are instructed to literally eat.

He is the sustenance of the soul, so that he even taught us to pray for it in what might be the most familiar prayer of Christendom, the Our Father (Matthew 6:8–13). In Matthew 6:11, Jesus says, "Give us this day our daily bread." I always wondered why Jesus was redundant here. "This day" and "daily" in the same sentence seemed strange.

The Douay-Rheims is the only translation that translates this repetition as "Give us this day our supersubstantial bread." The Greek word is *epiousios*, *epi-* meaning "super or hyper," *-ousios* meaning "substance." Somehow this "daily bread" is super bread!

This is exactly what Jesus meant when he said, "Whosoever eats my flesh and drinks my blood has eternal life, and I will raise him up at the last day. For my flesh is food indeed, and my blood is drink indeed…. It is the spirit that gives life, the flesh is of no avail; the words that I have spoken to you are spirit and life" (John 6:54–55, 63). As St. John Chrysostom says, "What then? Is it not real flesh? Yes, truly. In saying then that the flesh profits nothing, He does not speak of His own flesh, but that of the carnal hearer of His word."[5]

Because we did not have Eucharistic theology, as a non-Catholic, I (Sonja) was taught *spiritual* means "symbolic," but in what dictionary does *spiritual* mean "symbolic," or vice versa? In fact, to be a true antitype, the new manna must be *in all ways* superior to its type. The Old Testament manna wasn't symbolic; it was real enough to nourish them in the desert for forty years. How then can this new manna be symbolic?

Spiritual means "super- or hypernatural"; it means "more than just bread." Moses's daily manna fed the physical lives of God's people, but the Bread of Life, Jesus, feeds us himself—daily, supernatural, eternal life bread. Hallelujah!

When Jesus says, "The flesh profits nothing," he refers to our own flesh. The spirit that gives life is the Holy Spirit. The same Holy Spirit who incarnates the Lord Jesus in the womb of the Blessed Virgin Mary is the same Holy Spirit who changes bread and wine into the Body and Blood of our Lord Jesus Christ. The Lord that we receive in Holy Communion is the same Jesus that walked around almost two thousand years ago, the resurrected Lord. We receive the Body, Blood, soul, and divinity of our resurrected Lord when we receive Holy Communion. The seed of the resurrected life of Our Lord is planted in us. The Body of Our Lord can save (John 6:58). Glory!

Eucharist means "thanksgiving." The Church did not invent the Eucharist; she received it from Jesus on the night of his crucifixion and continues it to this day at his command, exactly as he gave it.

The early Church also retained the Old Testament understanding of remembrance as a participation, and called this sacrament "the breaking of bread." As St. Paul affirmed and the Catholic Church still teaches, Christ is truly present in the Eucharist (1 Corinthians 10:16–17). Our Holy Eucharist is in the presence of God through Christ,. But it is also the eternal presence of God, tabernacling with us in, with, and through Christ in his Church. The Eucharist is the daily, consistent continuation of God's command that there be perpetual bread of the presence in the tabernacle.

Jesus's presence in the Eucharist is the fulfillment and interpretation of all Old Testament bread. He feeds us himself. Better than manna, we can live forever with God by becoming one with him by eating this bread of the presence. "'Do this in remembrance of me.' We carry out this command of the Lord when we offer bread and wine which, by the power of the Holy Spirit and by the words of Christ, become the body and blood of Christ. Christ is really and mysteriously made *present*" (*CCC,* 1356–1357).

> The Eucharist is the memorial of Christ's Passover, that is, of the work of salvation accomplished through the life, death, and resurrection of Christ, a work made present by liturgical action. It is Christ himself, the eternal high priest of the new covenant who, acting through the ministry of the priests, offers the Eucharistic sacrifice. And it is the same Christ, really present under the species of bread and wine, who is the offering of the Eucharistic sacrifice. (*CCC,* 1409–1410)

Jesus is our new tabernacle, our new Moses, our new Lamb, our new Law, and our Bread of Life. Jesus was a prophet like Moses, only better. Moses died, but the New Testament tells us that Jesus is alive forever to make intercession for us. Jesus breaks the shackles of the bondage of sin. On life's journey to the promised land (heaven), he is our guide and provider, and his provision is the new manna to nourish the soul and restore the spirit.

There is one big difference between Jesus and Moses: Moses led the people to the Promised Land, but he wasn't allowed to enter himself. As wise and good as Moses was, even he had sinned. Jesus, on the other hand, is the perfect mediator, because he was innocent, without sin, and took our deserved punishment upon himself. He is waiting in heaven for all those who put their trust in him. When we see Jesus there, certainly Moses will be there too, as the one who knew and foretold his coming and trusted in him.

Let's Review
This is how God's New Testament people worship him.

- God is not schizophrenic but utterly consistent: *the "how" of the New Testament is built on the skeleton of the old.*
- *Jesus is the new and final tabernacle of worship.* The Church is his Body, built of "living stones."
- *Jesus is the new Moses,* prophet, priest, and king who leads us on a new exodus from the Egypt of sin to the last Promised Land of heaven.
- *New Testament worship should resemble both* Old Testament and heavenly worship.
- *Jesus is the final Passover Lamb* whose sacrifice takes away the sins of the world.
- *The New Testament law is the Gospel* of Christ, the law of love.
- *The sacrifice of the Mass is the "how"* of the New Testament.
- *The Eucharist is the source and summit of the Christian life* (*CCC,* 1324).

INVITATION

Jesus is the new Moses, bringing a new law. But Jesus isn't wrapped in flashing mists on cloud-capped, craggy Sinai in the middle of the barren desert. The earth doesn't quake so that the people tremble under his awful glory. Jesus doesn't thunder out commands, or write it all down in parchments and hand it over. Jesus doesn't teach like Moses or the prophets or the Pharisees or any other teacher we've ever known: "You have heard it said...but I say to you..."

Every utterance of this man is power. Not a syllable is lost. Nothing returns empty. Every vowel and consonant pushes forward with purpose and intent. It accomplishes what is spoken. And Jesus doesn't use words like a firehose to overwhelm and distance us in their collective onslaught. He simply pours himself all out like a stream in the desert, so the last drop of life-giving freshness trickles over a cracked-open, parched human race.

GOD PROMPT—LOVE THE WORD

Lectio—Listen

> Seeing the crowds, he went up on the mountain, and when he
> sat down his disciples came to him. And he opened his mouth
> and taught them, saying:
>
>> "Blessed are the poor in spirit, for theirs is the kingdom of
>> heaven.
>>
>> "Blessed are those who mourn, for they shall be comforted.
>>
>> "Blessed are the meek, for they shall inherit the earth.
>>
>> "Blessed are those who hunger and thirst for righteousness,
>> for they shall be satisfied.
>>
>> "Blessed are the merciful, for they shall obtain mercy.
>>
>> "Blessed are the pure in heart, for they shall see God.
>>
>> "Blessed are the peacemakers, for they shall be called sons
>> of God.
>>
>> "Blessed are those who are persecuted for righteousness'
>> sake, for theirs is the kingdom of heaven.
>>
>> "Blessed are you when men revile you and persecute you
>> and utter all kinds of evil against you falsely on my account.
>> "Rejoice and be glad, for your reward is great in heaven,
>> for so men persecuted the prophets who were before you"
>> (Matthew 5:1–10).

Oratio—Observe

How did it feel sitting on the springtime meadow grass dotted with
lilies in the quiet of early morning, catching the occasional whiff of
what strains the fishermen's nets as they are brought up from the
shores of the lake in the distance? What was it like as the human race
heard such radical things for the first time?

How did it feel to be part of that crowd? Did the grass sing? Did
the earth pound with the new truths, the new law inaugurated with
every word? No longer a matter of mere outward behavior, Jesus

revealed that holiness includes something deeper, something higher, something fuller. What was Jesus emphasizing?

If God is not schizophrenic but utterly consistent, why does Jesus come to us so differently from Moses? What does the springtime, pastoral Galilean setting communicate? What emotions play across Jesus's face as he eases his overflowing heart in the company of those wholly devoted to him? Are you amazed at every word, the cadence of each syllable? Why or why not?

Reread the passage from the Sermon on the Mount. As you read, think, "Do I believe him?"

What should you do now?

Meditatio—Verbalize

Dear Jesus, what a balm your words are to my soul, how strange and surprising their tenor. I see that you have suited yourself to the comprehension of earnest hearers, the way you repeat one thought over and over, laying it before me in a new form each time so I can appreciate nuance and subtlety. I sense how you long to be known and loved through the gentleness of your teachings. And yet how difficult they are!

You seem never too tired to prolong your instruction while my soul strains for your help to understand. Reflected in your words, as in a clear and spotless mirror, I see how backward I live from you. I see my prejudice, my preconceptions, my selfishness. That you seek to overthrow them all undoes me, and I am afraid of all you ask, even as the hope of it draws me to you. I pray for the grace and courage to live out this new law of love in all my duties today, especially the one you are pointing out to me here....

Contemplatio—Entrust

Maybe you want to offer thanksgiving for the gentleness with which your Savior approaches you.

chapter eight
The Why of the Bible

One of the issues I (Sonja) regularly speak on is the father wound. My father's critical spirit and aggressive parenting style instilled a deep experience of badness in me that made me feel unloved and unlovable. The only attention I seemed able to generate was negative, so I acted out.

Particularly in the weeks upon weeks of restriction and silent treatment while his face and warmth were turned away from me, I felt the isolation and darkness of being unloved because of my badness (a long-term result has been an ongoing terror of darkness and silence from God in prayer, but that's another abandonment story). I found any good attention was conditional on good behavior and performance, which I was unable to maintain, and was unrelated to who I was. As a child, this feeling motivated all sorts of misbehavior.

As an adult who left misbehavior behind but still felt unloved, I developed problems with rage (rebellion is my predominant fault),[1] depression, addictions, and hosts of other sins in an outward grasping for anything that made me feel powerful or happy.

I don't know about you, but the wound in my soul was a gaping, ravenous abyss of need. Nothing finite could fill it then, and nothing finite can fill it now. Only Jesus can satisfy the soul. As I began learning to live consciously in his love, I experienced round after round of painful circumstances that probed my woundedness and provoked my predominant fault. Satan exploited my wounds in innumerable, excruciating, creative ways.

But somehow through the Bible, like GPS, God rerouted my anxious, fearful, depressed wrong turns back to the road that led straight into his arms. I discovered the "why" of the Bible for myself within its pages: "For I am sure that neither death, nor life, nor angels, nor principalities, nor things present, nor things to come, nor powers, nor height, nor depth, nor anything else in all creation, will be able to separate us from the love of God in Christ Jesus our Lord" (Romans 8:38–39). God loves all he has made with a matchless, eternal love.

Perhaps one of the first issues confronting anyone who begins to read, study, and love the Bible is confusion regarding its meaning. Understanding the Bible's purpose explains to us why it was written and why we should read it. In a nutshell, the purpose of the Bible, its "why," is God's personal love, summarized so succinctly in John 3:16: "For God so loved the world that he gave his only begotten Son, that whoever believes in him should not perish but have eternal life."

The Catechism also provides insight on the "why" of the Bible:

Man is in search of God.... Even after losing through his sin his likeness to God, man remains an image of his Creator, and retains the desire for the one who calls him into existence. All religions bear witness to men's essential search for God.

God calls man first. Man may forget his Creator or hide far from his face; he may run after idols or accuse the deity of having abandoned him; yet the living and true God tirelessly calls each person to that mysterious encounter known as prayer. In prayer, the faithful God's initiative of love always comes first; our own first step is always a response. As God gradually reveals himself and reveals man to himself, prayer appears as a reciprocal call, a covenant drama. Through words and actions, this drama engages the heart. It unfolds throughout the whole history of salvation. (*CCC*, 2566–2567)

As we said in chapter three, the sacred Scriptures are "his-story," a sort of five-act play, if you will: the creation and fall; the story of Israel, the race of Jesus; the story of Jesus; the story of the Church; and the new creation. Knowing, understanding, and adjusting our lives to "his-story" can save us. It offers abundant life, wholeness, and peace.

But this salvation is not merely relief from some sort of punitive judicial sentence. Salvation is unto something, or more accurately, unto someone. God is just judge, but he is also Father, so his judgments are fatherly. The consummate fatherhood of God foreshadowed in Abraham and revealed in Christ is said to be the most revolutionary reality of the whole Bible.

Covenants teach us why God does all he does in people and times and places, and why he asks us to do the "how" of worship. Biblical covenants show us why God the Father loves and fathers his family throughout salvation history, beginning with Adam and Eve.

Even before the Fall, God had a plan to ensure his beloved creation could remain with him forever. History is the story of that glorious plan, working until the end of time, through a series of seven covenants. History, specifically salvation history, is the sweeping story of that working until the end of time through a series of covenants, so that the Bible tells the love story of human salvation from the beginning of time to its final conclusion.

St. Irenaeus, who was the bishop of Lyon in late second-century France, said that to understand "the divine program and economy for the salvation of humanity" we have to understand God's "several covenants with humanity" and also "the special character of each covenant."[2] The key to understanding the "why" of the Bible lies in understanding covenant.

An Exchange of Persons
According to one Catholic encyclopedia, a covenant is "a solemn promise, fortified by an oath, concerning future action. The oath

might be expressed in words or in a symbolic action."[3]

In Hebrew, the word for "covenant" or "oath" means to "seven oneself." A covenant is not simply a legal contract; it is an exchange of persons, or a family bond, as Dr. Scott Hahn has called it.[4] More than an impersonal legal contract in which two parties agree to an exchange of goods and services, a covenant binds persons together beyond the mere contractual agreement.

In a covenant, God swears the complete and total gift of himself to us and we reciprocate that gift in love that is free, faithful, total, and fruitful. Such love is rooted in the mutual sacrifice of complete self-donation, because God does not hold back any of his love from us.

Each biblical covenant involves a series of important elements. An oath or swearing is involved in an invocation of God's name, for example, "I swear to God." Covenants are initiated by God and offered to a particular person who is representative of all in an exchange of persons: "I am yours, and you are mine," or "I will be your God, and you will be my people."

Each covenant carries a sign as a permanent memorial of its validity. Covenants illustrate the relationship between God and his people by including an increasingly larger circle of relationship than the covenant before. As each concentric circle is contained in the next, they are each permanently valid. Every covenant foreshadows the final covenant in Christ and his new creation. Covenants involve built-in blessings and curses. Finally, all covenants progressively reveal more of God's complete self-gift to humanity proceeding from Trinitarian communion, until the final covenant in which he reveals himself as the Bridegroom of his Church.

Have you ever wondered why God created in seven days rather than just one? In addition to swearing an oath, seven is the number of divine perfection in the Bible. By creating in six days and resting on the seventh, God "sevened" himself to all he made, thereby inviting us all—cosmos, angels, humanity—into covenant with him and swearing himself to us as our Father. Following the pattern of the seven days of creation, there are also seven covenants of salvation history.

ADAMIC COVENANT

Like the two complementary halves of a single marriage, the first chapters of Genesis give us two complementary accounts of creation and two complementary parts to the first covenant. In the first chapter, we see God as Almighty—God simply spoke, and it was done. He created in six days and "sevened" himself to it all on the seventh.

In the second account, located in chapter two, we find God's personal, intimate involvement in creation. The word "formed" is used repeatedly in this chapter, and it is the term for a potter's shaping of pots. In this context, it is used to describe God molding and shaping a human body from mud and clay.

I (Sonja) remember watching a potter throw a bowl for the first time. The rhythmic sound of the rotating wheel was nearly hypnotic. The potter was bent almost fully over the clay, completely absorbed in carefully but firmly applying proper pressure to make the clay respond. It was such an elemental, physical, muddy occupation.

When God finished his work in creation he "gave" the whole pristine lot to the man and woman (Genesis 1:26–28) as a gift. It awes us that God would do that. That he would go to such extravagant lengths to create a universe and planet teeming with diversity and life—from solar systems to plankton—and then give it, completely, to someone else to manage. What are your thoughts about that? Would you hand over something you invented and created from nothing entirely to someone else?

The seventh day of creation received God's special blessing (Genesis 2:2–3). God blessed it. Depending on which version of the

Scriptures you use, you may also see the term "sanctified." This means to set it aside for special use and is also what the word *holy* means. But he also "rested." Because God is uncreated Spirit, the term *rest* is a representation of God in our familiar human form. Theologians use the term *anthropomorphism* for describing God with human forms or attributes.

Later, once the Law was given on Mount Sinai, the people would participate in this "sanctification" and Sabbath blessing-rest on a weekly basis, but it was here, in the beginning, that God's Sabbath became the sign of God's covenant with creation.

After God created the universe, he created rest. *Sabbath* means "rest." His resting made it a permanent covenant, the oath day. Then he instituted the Sabbath as a sign for the people that would there-after illustrate their desire to share in the covenant.

Keeping a true Sunday rest is like saying, "Yes, Lord! I want you as my Lord. You formed me for love, to walk with you in an intimate relationship. I receive you, Body and Blood. Take me to yourself, once again. Make my earthly marriage a glowing depiction of your eternal, sacrificial love."

When our relationship with God gets to these heights, we are experiencing the intimate, eternal, ecstatic rest for which we were created. This is beatitude, the paradise of Adam's covenant undefiled.

In these first chapters of Genesis, we see that everything was made by God in seven days, that he made it all for man, and that it was good—even very good! In Hebrew, the name Adam is used to refer to the whole human race, so this covenant is really a covenant with all people in all times, and the one from which all the other covenants spring. What does it mean for you, personally, that God has cove-nanted himself to you? Adam, as first and head of humanity, became the steward of God's creation.

Just after this, God did something else that was especially touching. In a second action that is also covenant, God established for Adam a particular relationship. God fell on Adam in what amounts to "an ecstasy," according to the Septuagint, and using a rib, made or built a wife for Adam.

In Genesis 2:21–25, two different words are used in God's creation of the first two humans. Does it seem odd that he would "form" Adam, but "build" Eve? Doesn't the expansion of one small part into a complete body make sense in today's understanding of molecular structure and DNA? God created Adam and Eve to be joined together as one flesh: "Then the man said, 'This at last is bone of my bones and flesh of my flesh; she shall be called Woman, because she was taken out of Man.' Therefore a man leaves his father and his mother and cleaves to his wife, and they become one flesh" (Genesis 2:23–24).

In a tender act of friendship, God made Adam a wife, bone of his bones and flesh of his flesh—a mirror of himself, yet so different!— a perfect complement. In doing so, he also established Adam as a husband in a covenant, a permanent marital relationship in order to illustrate his own intimate relationship to creation and marriage. God is our husband. The Church has always understood this account of the creation of Eve to point to something forthcoming in the distant future.

The first marriage and every one after that all point to Jesus as head of the Church, his bride (Ephesians 5:22–33). We know because St. Paul quotes Genesis 2:24 in teaching Christ as Bridegroom to the Church, his bride. There's another interesting reinforcement of the link in Ephesians 5:30. As Eve was flesh of Adam's flesh, we are "members of His body, of His flesh and bones," and Jesus gives us his Body in the Eucharist. In exchange, we give ourselves to him in fecund love and obedience. The glory of marriage is indeed splendid to the point of breathtaking. Do you see why the Church can never advocate divorce, a feminine priesthood, contraception, or homosexual marriage?

Because of the "sevening" God did regarding the Adamic covenant, not only did God covenant himself to creation, but he also covenanted himself to marriage. Throughout the ages of history, people, even godly people, abused and disfigured this elevated intent for marriage, but Jesus upheld and even strengthened the original design in Matthew 19:3–12. When there are historical questions about marriage, its intent, and its sacredness, Jesus elevates it to a sacrament, a permanent covenant that illustrates his martial relationship to the Church, and that actually confers grace to the participants through Jesus himself and his sacrifice (cf. Ephesians 5:22–33).

We are all navigating the definition of marriage and the issues surrounding marriage in our society today—loving marriage, unsatisfying marriage, abusive marriage, divorce, remarriage, gay marriage, cohabitation, contraception, and so-called women priests. But the first scriptural covenant illustrates the ancient reality that whether single or married, lay or religious, as part of the Church, we are all created for intimate, marital communion with a human spouse, and/ or with God himself.

In every Old Testament covenant, there is a steward of the covenant, or the person with whom God made the covenant, whose role is its management or administration. In the first covenant, that person and steward was Adam, whose role was husband. There is also always a covenant relationship that carries the covenant forth into history and forever after illustrates the relationship of the covenant God made with that person. The Adamic Covenant relationship was marriage. But in every Old Testament covenant, there is also a covenant sign to show participation in and loyalty to the covenant. In every covenant, this sign was something the people participated in to show their fidelity to the covenant.

Covenant Steward	Adam
Covenant Role	Husband
Covenant Relationship	Marriage
Covenant Sign	Sabbath

NOAHIC COVENANT

Don't you think there is something magical and wondrous about rainbows that even their scientific explanation cannot diminish? Practically every picture I (Sonja) drew as a little girl was of a house with flowers and a rainbow over it. Even as a child I sensed the hope that a rainbow speaks.

It's no mistake that the Church follows the Scriptures in elevating hope to a theological virtue. Basically, that means it's a virtue you need supernatural help to practice or have at all. And don't we know it. Life is hard. So hard, that it's very easy to get cynical. Fruitlessness, broken promises, betrayals, failures, unrealized dreams, they all conspire to discourage us. We are tempted to quit. We no longer wonder. We stop reaching. We tend toward bitterness.

We need a special grace to hope. Hope is what God's covenant with Noah is about. If you are in need of a special infusion of hope from God, we believe you'll find it in the Noahic covenant account in Genesis, chapters six through nine.

Genesis 5:29 tells us Noah's name means "consolation," or "rest." We find that both strange and comforting. Strange, since Noah witnessed the most dreadful catastrophe and disturbance that had ever happened in the world to that point. Interesting, because part of the Adamic covenant also included rest. You might want to circle Noah's name in your Bible and write rest beside it.

Genesis 6:1–7 tells us the reason for the catastrophe is abuse of the marriage covenant. Mankind has broken its first covenant with God.

The sacred marriage relationship that illustrated God's great love for his people has been completely defiled, and men became "violent" with one another, a Hebrew euphemism for murder.

Before his judgment fell, God again initiated a covenant—an exchange of persons. Like the one he made with Adam, this covenant reflects a promise God makes to the individual, all humanity through the individual, and it takes the form of both Adam's social relationship, and Noah's social relationship: a family.

Notice also the contrast between the evil men who walked the Earth and Noah, who walked with God. In Noah lies the hope of all human history after him. Had there not been a man and a family who by God's grace remained genuinely righteous in the midst of the wickedness of their day, God's new beginning would have omitted all of us.

Does this thought give you hope when you consider the times we live in? It does for us. We know that we can pray for God's grace to remain loyal to him in our own violent, graceless age, and rely on his grace to help preserve our children and our families. That is a great hope.

Noah obeyed God and built a floating box, sealed against leaks, for a flood, when it had never yet rained. In the genealogy of Genesis 5, there are ten generations, all but one over 850 years. In all that time, it had not rained. We think of the ark as a boat, which is designed for conveyance. But the ark was built to simply float on the water. Imagine the gossip Noah's obedience provoked. Have you ever been obedient to God and felt silly or embarrassed for it?

The flood waters fell downwards and surged upwards, remaining on the earth for 150 days. That's five months underwater. All living flesh and foliage outside the lifesaving ark died (Genesis 6:17).

It wasn't anywhere near the scale of the great deluge, but I (Sonja) remember the fear and destruction of the Nashville flood of 2010.

We live far enough north that our experience was more of the flash-flood variety than the rising, sustained flooding further south. But it was certainly something to behold. I remember wondering how in the world it could rain so much and watching the radar with awe, realizing there was so much more to come. We live on the other side of a creek, so we were unable to leave our house for several days. For months afterward, we found parts of our bridge downstream. Our neighbors' camper, cars, lawn mower, and the contents of several peoples' outbuildings were deposited by the creekside for miles.

In 1 Peter 3:19–21, St. Peter presents Noah's flood account as a type of Christian baptism. Just like the flood cleansed the earth of its evil and violence unto the opportunity for godliness and new life, baptism cleanses the soul of sin unto purity and new, even eternal, life.

The Church has always seen Noah's ark as a symbol of the Church, through which the sacrament of baptism is administered. St. Augustine even drew a parallel between Adam's rib, the door in the side of the boat from which Noah's family and the animals reentered the earth, and the side of Christ from which the water gushed and the Church was born. As Noah was saved through the flood from the earthly destruction of sin, baptism saves us from the eternal destruction of sin.

Noah, his family, and all the animals left the ark as the only breathing entities on the earth. Immediately, Noah built an altar and offered a sacrifice, entering into a covenant with God. Why do you think he did this? How grateful are you for your baptism?

In the covenant God made with Noah and his family, God promised to never again destroy mankind through a flood, and the rainbow was his constant reminder and sign (Genesis 9:8–17).

Covenant Steward	Noah
Covenant Role	Father
Covenant Relationship	Family
Covenant Sign	Rainbow

Have you ever considered that you *never* have to sin again? Your baptism was a death to sin and its power to make you sin. The tendency to sin will be with us until death, but living in sin is a choice. Sometimes it is motivated by deep wounds, but it is still a choice. You have only to walk in grace by calling on the Holy Spirit, that dove-like harbinger and power of hope, for help in doing the difficult work of holiness. This is new life. Like Adam's, God's covenant with Noah was permanent, signified by the startling rainbow that appears after a summer thunderstorm. Mercy. Grace. Redemption. Hope.

ABRAHAMIC COVENANT

Of all the covenant fathers, Abraham is one of the two I (Sonja) identify with the most, because God has led me in very similar ways. I remind myself of God's dealings with Abraham all the time. The accounts give me comfort and help me persevere.

In the poetic passage that tells us of it, God initiates a covenant with Abram that begins with a command to leave his land, his clan, and his family, and travel toward a promise. In ancient times, this was simply not done, as his father's house was where a man assumed responsibility and leadership as tribal chief when his father died. Leaving would have been a hurtful, insulting renunciation of everything Abram had ever known. Only a landless fugitive would have left an ancestral home and wandered around in that day and time. The difficulty of the demand to leave everything behind was only intensified by the fact that Abram was traveling to a location that wasn't even defined until he got there.

Although Abram would not lead a tribe in his own country, the second half of this poetic covenant served as a promise to replace all Abram would give up by following God (Genesis 12:1–4). There are, significantly, seven parts to Abraham's covenant.

Abram will leave behind all he knows, but God will eventually make a nation of him and the new tribe created through him and his obedience, the Hebrew nation.

God will bless Abram. God's blessing is the warmth of his pleasure, his pronouncement of what is very good.

God will give Abram a great name. That one's name would endure long after one's lifetime was a supreme honor. We know him today as Abraham, our father of faith.

God will honor Abram in such ways so he can be a blessing to others. This phrase is both a command and a promise, as all of God's word is. That we can be a blessing is always why God blesses us. Elements five and six form a poetic couplet and are closely related. Because God's blessing rests on Abram forever in covenant, those who follow in Abram's footsteps are automatically blessed, and those who don't forfeit blessing entirely. The absence of God's blessing is in itself a curse.

The final element of the covenant is perhaps the most sweeping. All the families on the earth will be blessed through Abram, obviously a reference to the Christ who will someday come.

Many years after the initial covenant, God reaffirms his promises and changes Abram's name to Abraham (Genesis 17:1–8), and the "exalted father" becomes "father of many." As a perpetual sign of participation in the covenant, God commands that all the children that follow from Abraham's lineage and tribe should be circumcised (Genesis 9–27).

Covenant Steward	Abram
Covenant Role	Patriarch
Covenant Relationship	Tribe
Covenant Sign	Circumcision

By the time of the Mosaic covenant, Abraham's children—the whole congregation of God's people—numbered around a million souls, counting women and children. And all the twelve tribes of Israel had been slaves to Egypt for half a millennium.

MOSAIC COVENANT

All the controversy with Pharaoh was about letting the Hebrew people go to Mount Sinai to offer sacrifices to God, and God was determined that they should be allowed to do so. The book of Exodus tells the story of the Mosaic covenant. Their Exodus had drawn them out of Egypt under Moses. Suddenly they were a nation. A nation with whom God was about to call to covenant with him.

Before God initiated the covenant, he reminded the people of all he had already done on their behalf. If they obeyed him and kept the covenant, God promised to make them his special treasure. He would lavish special attention on them and make them a kingdom of priests and a holy nation. Israel would become entirely unique from every other nation in existence at that time and forevermore, because of its relationship with the living God. All the other nations would learn of the Lord God through them, and they would attract and lead others to correctly worship him. The people readily agreed (Exodus 19:3–9).

The night they were to leave Egypt, the Lord gave Moses some very specific instructions for what would become the sign of participation in the Mosaic covenant, the Passover. The Passover would be a communal meal. They were to publicly slaughter a perfect lamb, spread its blood on their doorposts, and eat it, roasted, with unleavened bread. If they did not follow these directions to a T, the death angel would not pass over their home on his sweep through Egypt, and their firstborns would die along with all the rest in the country (Exodus 11–12).

It was at the foot of Mount Sinai that a man with a heart for righteousness was called to lead a nation back to worship. It was at the top of this mountain that Moses received the Ten Commandments through which he would judge and instruct the people in righteousness, and instructions for proper worship in the tabernacle that would be built at its base. Moses was faithful. The new nation of God made it to the place he had wanted them to go from the beginning, and they would do at the foot of the mountain what he desired all along: worship. The nation would remember this event forever through the annual Passover meal.

Covenant Steward	Moses
Covenant Role	Judge
Covenant Relationship	Nation
Covenant Sign	Passover

Davidic Covenant

Eventually the nation of Israel rejected God's leadership through the priests, judges, and prophets and wanted a king like their neighboring nations. A young warrior-poet-shepherd boy whose heart was known and chosen by God would be the next covenant steward. David was anointed and then formed in the crucible of persecution for fifteen years before he ascended the throne. David reigned for forty years, unifying the Israelites under one ruler and conquering surrounding nations through near-constant military campaigns. Throughout his reign, he constantly inquired of the Lord for permission to act.

This tender, intimate relationship with the Lord, as he said, "The Lord is my shepherd…" (Psalm 23:1), was the key to David's successful reign. David demonstrated the importance of his religious convictions to all Israel very early when one of the first things he undertook as king was the transfer of the Ark of the Covenant to Jerusalem, the holy city (2 Samuel 6).

David installs the Ark in Jerusalem, and then he longs to build a "house" or permanent temple for it to rest in. But the Lord has another idea, saying to David,

> The Lord declares to you that the Lord will make you a house. When your days are fulfilled and you lie down with your fathers, I will raise up your offspring after you, who shall come forth from your body, and I will establish his kingdom. He shall build a house for my name, and I will establish the throne of his kingdom forever. I will be his father, and he shall be my son. When he commits iniquity, I will chasten him with the rod of men, with the stripes of the sons of men; but I will not take my steadfast love from him, as I took it from Saul, whom I put away from before you. And your house and your kingdom shall be made sure for ever before me; your throne shall be established forever. (2 Samuel 7:11–16)

Although it was a worthwhile, lofty ambition, David would not build the Lord a house; the Lord would build David a house. This term *house* is a euphemism for a royal dynasty. The sign of the covenant would be an eternal throne.

This is so like God, isn't it? Our hearts yearn to do great things for him, out of thanksgiving and praise and joy, and yet he simply awaits the opportunity to do great things for us. In this tribute rests the Davidic Covenant.

Covenant Steward	David
Covenant Role	King
Covenant Relationship	Kingdom
Covenant Sign	Throne

Through all the triumphs and tragedies of David's reign as king over the kingdom of God's people, God was acting in the national and personal events of his people in order to accomplish his will. The Lord gave David a glimpse of his ultimate will in the promises of the Davidic Covenant, promising him an eternal dynasty, an eternal throne, and an eternal kingdom. Ultimately, a righteous King greater than David was coming. He would be David's "son," and would rule from David's throne forever. This promised king is Jesus.

THE NEW COVENANT

"God communicates himself to man gradually. He prepares him to welcome by stages the supernatural Revelation that is to culminate in the person and mission of the incarnate Word, Jesus Christ" (*CCC*, 53). Jesus is the new Adam (1 Corinthians 15:45–49), the new Noah (Ephesians 5:22–33), the new Isaac (Genesis 22:8 with Exodus 12), the new Moses (John 6:30–71), and the new David (Luke 1:31–33 with John 1:49).

Notice how God's family form progressed with each of God's six covenants—man and wife, family, tribe, nation, kingdom, universal worldwide kingdom. I (Sonja) used to view the Church as tangential to history and all that is occurring in the world, sort of an afterthought if you will, but the opposite is true: all that occurs in the world is centered on what God is doing in, with, and through the Church. What God has done and is doing through history is not only building up man's relationship to him using signs and other humans, he is revealing more and more of himself to us with each and every covenant, until at last he has revealed himself fully in Jesus

Christis.[5] Sadly, man broke each covenant and had to endure the curses of forfeit associated with each one. But God has been true to each one of his covenants with us, and that is really good news for us all.

Many years after David, the prophets foretold a new, complete, final covenant. "But this is the covenant which I will make with the house of Israel after those days," promised the Lord. "I will put my law within them, and I will write it upon their hearts" (cf. Jerimiah 31:33). Ezekiel prophesied it would be an eternal covenant (Ezekiel 37:26). Isaiah was shown its universal character, so "that [his] salvation may reach to the ends of the earth" (Isaiah 49:6). In what is called a Servant Song for its prophetic nature regarding the Messiah, Isaiah also saw that the new covenant would be a *person*: "I have given you as a covenant to the people, a light to the nations." (Isaiah 42:6).

The prophesied new covenant is the master theme of the New Testament that it is named for. When Paul explained the institution of the Eucharist at the Last Supper, his language indicates a whole body of Tradition, teachings that he received from Christ and delivered to the Corinthians, even repeating Christ's own words: "For I received from the Lord what I also delivered to you, that the Lord Jesus on the night when he was betrayed took bread, and when he had given thanks, he broke it, and said, 'This is my body which is for you. Do this in remembrance of me'" (1 Corinthians 11:23–24). The theme is reinforced in the Letter to the Hebrews: "It follows that it is a greater covenant for which Jesus has become our guarantee" (Hebrews 7:22). Christ himself is the new covenant between God and his people (from the Latin *convenire*, meaning "to agree," "to come together").

Indeed, it is the new "coming together" of God and his people in the person of Christ, our new covenant, that is the "why" of the New Testament, and is that which forges the relationship between what is sacrament and what is covenant.

A Sacramental Economy

Only after understanding the self-donation basis of covenant can we approach the deeper meaning of the New Testament's sacramental economy. In the Old Testament, God gave himself in covenant through increasing stages of self-donation, first to a couple, then a family, tribe, nation, and kingdom. But there was no grace invested in the people's observances of their side of the covenants to affect the holiness required to "come together" permanently or eternally with God, which was the longing of his heart and the "why" of all of his-story. Only in, with, and through Christ could the observances commanded become grace-filled and therefore efficacious and salvific.

What connection might this have with the sacraments? The Latin word for oath is *sacramentum*, from which we get the word *sacrament*. Christ instituted seven of these *sacramentum*. So Christ instituted seven covenant-making, and covenant-renewing oaths, each an increasing self-donation: Baptism, Eucharist, Reconciliation, Confirmation, Marriage, Holy Orders, and Anointing of the Sick. Like other oaths, the sacraments involve the invoking of God's name, an exchange of persons, permanence, and blessings and curses of forfeiture.

At the beginning of Mass, we invoke God's name: "In the name of the Father, Son, and Holy Spirit." We have therefore put ourselves under oath to fulfill the terms of the new covenant. When the priest offers the Eucharist, saying, "The body of Christ" and "The blood of Christ," and we respond, "Amen," and receive the Lord into our very bodies, we enter into an exchange of persons.

He gives himself to us, and through our "amen" and reception of the Body and Blood of Christ, we give ourselves to him in covenant. Literally. Hallelujah? He gave himself up unto death for us so that we might receive him. So, too, we are called to give ourselves up unto death so that he might receive us. This exchange of the totality of the divine person of Christ and the totality of ourselves is to be permanent.

The most spectacular reality of the new covenant is that sin no longer prevents our "coming together" with God. This is why the Gospel is truly "good news." Throughout our lives, we must call upon the blessings of the Lord to aid us in fulfilling the covenant. But when we do not keep the covenant, when we do not live a life worthy of the calling to which we have been called in Christ (Ephesians 4:1), we automatically forfeit the blessings of the new covenant. By nature God cannot break covenant, but we can and often do.

St. Paul warns of this reality when he says: "Whoever, therefore, eats the bread or drinks the cup of the Lord in an unworthy manner will be guilty of profaning the body and blood of the Lord. Let a man examine himself, and so eat of the bread and drink of the cup. For anyone who eats and drinks without discerning the body eats and drinks judgment upon himself." (1 Corinthians 11:27–29). Whether through no-fault ignorance or conscious rejection, such profaning and judgment is why non-Catholics and non-believers are not permitted at the Eucharistic table until they have been instructed in its solemnity.

In the sacraments, we swear an oath to God that we will live faithfully and give ourselves completely to him, Sunday through Saturday, in the boardroom, the family room, and the bedroom. There can be no picking and choosing which part of our lives we give to Christ, because he gave himself completely, broken and spilled out, first on Calvary and now in the sacraments.

We are part of the couple, the family, the tribe, the nation, the worldwide (catholic, meaning universal) new covenant kingdom. The new covenant in Christ binds God to his people, and his people to one another, with a future promise of redemption even for creation (cf. Ephesians 2:11–22).

The Bible begins with the story of the creation of the world, and ends with the passing away of heaven and Earth and the coming down of "a new heaven and a new earth." This "new heaven and new earth" will constitute the seventh covenant, new and everlasting (Revelation 21:1), at which time all things will have been truly and permanently made new in Christ (Revelation 21:5). Amen and hallelujah!

Let's Review

This is why the Bible is a called a love letter from God.

- *The Bible, start to finish, is a book of covenant.*
- *A covenant is a permanent exchange of persons* in love.
- *Seven is the number of divine completion* or perfection.
- *There are seven biblical covenants.*
- *Each biblical covenant is an increasing self-donation and self-revelation of God:* creation and marriage, family, tribe, nation, kingdom, world. The last covenant will commence at the end of time.
- *Jesus in his person is the new and final covenant* in which all things are made new and "come together" with God.
- *Jesus instituted seven Christian sacraments*, or covenants, that administer and affect saving grace in our souls and equip us for complete self-donation to God.

Invitation

The choices we make shape our lives forever. Our decisions, if guided by the Holy Spirit, change us permanently in ways that draw us deeper into the mystery of God's Trinitarian life. Many would describe the outcomes of these decisions as matters of fate, but I (Deacon Harold) see them more as matters of faith, of God's loving guidance, beneficence, and continuous involvement in our lives through which his divine action plan is evidenced, just like it is in the Bible. One of the most significant moments in my life was my decision to attend St. Benedict's preparatory school in Newark, New Jersey.

St. Benedict's is an oasis in the desert: it is a place where the life, mission, and spirit of Benedictine monasticism flourish amidst the poverty, noise, and pollution of the inner city. It is a place where the Gospel is taught by word and by example, where young boys become young men, where pain and despair give way to joy and hope. It was here that I developed a lifelong love for the Liturgy of the Hours, and a deep admiration of and respect for monastic life in the Benedictine tradition.

My initial visit to the monastery came about by accident. Early in the fall semester of my freshman year, Abbot Melvin addressed the students during the morning convocation and asked us to consider becoming monks. It was the only time during my four years that I remember the abbot addressing the entire student body. Later that morning, while speaking with another student about it, my freshman religion teacher, Fr. Matthew—who overheard my comments— asked if I was serious about visiting the monastery. I told him that I was, and he introduced me to Brother Thomas, who introduced me to the abbot. I was invited to attend dinner and Vespers one evening. Later, I was invited to stay for a weekend. By my sophomore year, I was staying for a week or more at a time.

In many ways, these were the best four years of my life. I loved staying in the monastery and I always looked forward to my next visit. My time in the monastery as a high school student strengthened the faith foundation laid by my mother and would serve me well during my college years. The monks taught me about the centrality of prayer and the meaning of work. My appreciation of and love for the sacrifice of the Mass and sacred Scripture grew deeper during this period. The daily recitation of the Divine Office, together with active engagement in lectio divina, engendered a regimented and systematic approach to prayer, reading, and contemplation that I still follow to this day. I realize now more than ever that my time in the monastery was a great blessing. I've received a great gift for which I am deeply and eternally grateful to Almighty God and to the monks of Newark Abbey.

After college, I became more and more open to the idea of joining the monastery and—despite my best efforts to suppress and deny what I was feeling—the idea never really left me. I sought out a spiritual advisor and began reading about Benedictine life. I also spent a lot of time reading the various works of Thomas Merton. After a year of prayer, conversation, and discernment, I decided to write the abbot and formally request admission to the monastery.

I entered the monastery as a postulant and left soon afterward. My mother had open-heart surgery and needed lots of help at home. Since my parents were divorced and I was the oldest, I felt it necessary to take a three-month leave of absence until my mother had sufficiently recovered.

I met Colleen—the woman who would become my wife—while I was out of the monastery. After two years, we became very close. When she moved to California to pursue graduate studies, I decided to join her a few months later thinking that God was taking me in the direction of marriage and family. After about six months, having not felt a strong desire to be married and have a family despite our deepening relationship, I began to think about the monastery once again. When I told Colleen what I was feeling, she was confused, angry, and disappointed. I realize now I made the mistake of not confronting my feelings about the monastic life in a more direct manner before moving across the country. I thought that once I was far enough away from the monastery, the desire to become a monk would diminish, but it did not. I didn't leave the monastery because I did not like monastic life; in fact, there were many things about it that I missed very much.

I needed to make a decision once and for all—to try and determine God's will for my life: am I supposed to be a monk or get married? I immediately made arrangements to move into a local Benedictine monastic community near Palo Alto, California, to discern.

Looking back, I can see that I was afraid. I never seriously considered getting married before I met Colleen, and the thought of being married frightened me. The monastery was a place where I felt safe and unafraid, which are not good reasons for joining a monastic community. The monastery is a place where the monk gives up everything in this life in order to have everything in the next. It is a place where the monk empties himself so that he can be filled with God alone. The monk lives in poverty and silence so that, enriched by a life of prayer, he can hear God loud and clear in the inner depths of his being. Is this the kind of life God was calling me to? If not, then why am I so attracted to it? God was certainly leading and directing me toward something, but what was it? I realized that I could not allow my decision to be guided by fear. After months of discernment that included Eucharistic Adoration and spiritual direction, I knew that God was calling me to be a husband and father.

My greatest revelation during that time was seeing the intimate relationship between marriage and the Eucharist. I came to understand that the married couple, as the image of the Trinitarian family on earth, is transformed more and more into the likeness of Christ each time they unite themselves to the living God, becoming one-flesh with him in the Eucharist.

I began to get it. I was finally able to envision a nexus between my married life and my spiritual life. I now cherish my role as head of the family, that is, as the chief servant of my wife and children. I understand that my relationship with God and my family must always come first above all else. Families are a special witness to God's loving plan in the world and the fertile ground for future generations of Catholics.

During a recent trip to the East Coast, I had an opportunity to revisit Newark Abbey. Once again, I prayed and ate with the men whom I had admired so much for most of my life (and still do!). It felt great. I began to wonder what life would have been like if God would have led me back to the monastery. *What would life be like if I had persevered in and dedicated myself to the monastic life?* I thought. After all, these monks played such an important role in my spiritual formation and development. I received from them a deep love of prayer, work, and silence, which have been tremendous blessings in my life. I would not be the person I am today if it were not for them.

After I said my good-byes and started driving toward the airport, I smiled as I thought about my wife and children, and how much I love them. I couldn't wait to get home.

God Prompt—LOVE the Word
Lectio—Listen

Be subject to one another out of reverence for Christ. Wives, be subject to your husbands, as to the Lord. For the husband is the head of the wife as Christ is the head of the church, his body, and is himself its Savior....

Husbands, love your wives, as Christ loved the church and gave himself up for her, that he might sanctify her, having cleansed her by the washing of water with the word, that he might present the church to himself in splendor, without spot or wrinkle or any such thing, that she might be holy and without blemish.... Even so husbands should love their wives as their own bodies. "For this reason a man shall leave his father and mother and be joined to his wife, and the two shall become one flesh." This mystery is a profound one, and I am saying that it refers to Christ and the church. (Ephesians 5:21–32)

Oratio—Observe

Our primary vocation as men and women is the same: to become self-gift. We give ourselves in love to God and to one another. We are, in fact, to become increasingly like God, who, in his very essence, is self-gift: three persons giving themselves eternally in love to each other.

The great sign of Ephesians 5 is the marriage relationship as the mysterious reflection of that between Christ and his Church. Christ is the Bridegroom. The Church is the bride. He lays down his life for her, and in doing so makes her holy.

In giving himself completely to the souls entrusted to him, a husband reflects Christ to his wife, and in some powerfully mysterious way contributes to her holiness and that of their children.

St. John Paul II said that holiness is always expressed through the body.[6] Jesus teaches us this lesson when he pronounced the most masculine words ever spoken, "This is my body, which is given up for you." His was the gift of self through the body, not just in the Eucharist or crucifixion, but even through his whole life as a man.

Meditatio—Verbalize

Dear Lord, instill in my heart the desire to understand and love you more, especially through this passage. May I respond to your will for my life.

How does this reading make me feel? Lighthearted? Heavyhearted? I may be very much at peace, happy to be here. Equally, I may be frustrated, worried, or angry. I acknowledge how I really am. It is the real me that the Lord loves.

Conversation requires talking and listening. As I talk to Jesus, may I also learn to be still and listen. What is Jesus saying to me?

Contemplatio—Entrust

I picture the welcome in his eyes and the warmth of his commitment to me in his smile as he gazes on me. I imagine placing myself fully in his care, abandoning myself to him, knowing that he always wants what is best for me.

chapter nine
Which Voice Is His?

When I (Sonja) began making my way into full communion with the Church, I felt some resentment toward my Baptist roots and even toward God, as though he had withheld the "good stuff" from me, or had messed up with my religious upbringing and finally detoured me to Catholicism as a fix, rather than having a real plan. As terrified as I was to step off the Protestant cliff into the theological ocean of Catholicism, a careful inventory of the Holy Spirit's tireless leadership up to that point made the jump exhilarating for several important reasons.

Although at the time I did not recognize it as such, the Holy Spirit led me through a spiritual review, of sorts. Before the Easter Vigil I was received into the Church, just as God did for the Israelites when they were about to finally enter the Promised Land, and I was invited to remember all the foundational gifts my Baptist roots had instilled in me.

As the book of Deuteronomy recounts in the Israelites' review, I too surveyed the ground I had covered and the spiritual markers of my life. Had the Old Testament liturgical structure really been deliberate preparation for Catholic worship all along, rather than something like a hard-drive crash that required complete replacement with the New Testament, as I had been taught? Was he using that realization to show me all my happily meandering Baptist roads and Protestant signposts had been a purposeful leading to this Catholic precipice all along? What a shocking possibility!

I first heard about Jesus in my Baptist mother's womb. She gave me Bible picture books before I could talk and kept me in an age-appropriate supply of Bible story books. At a sweltering outdoor revival, I was challenged to "come sinner, come home," as the old invitational song says, to repent of my sins and trust him with all my heart. After clutching the back of a wooden church pew with sweaty hands, I walked the aisle and gave my pitiful nine-year-old heart to Jesus at church camp and regularly repented of my backsliding on my knees at the altar call.

Evangelical teachers disciplined me in memorizing Bible verses, singing songs, and building a vocabulary with which to praise and pray to God. Under their instruction, I learned the simplicity of real faith, to view him as Father, and stop trying to earn what is totally gift. Under my Baptist pastors and mentors, I experienced the Bible as the living Word of God for the first time. Through Bible drills and summer camps, they fed me Scripture until it became part of my own thoughts and sentences.

From towers of Baptist holiness, I learned divine love is sacrificial, and to grow in sacrifice is to grow in Christ. I was challenged to pray first but always to trust that he always answered prayers with a "yes," "no," or "wait," and to thank him ahead of time for the answer because it was surely the best answer he could give me.

I learned to hear him and follow him no matter what or where. I learned that "All Scripture is inspired by God and profitable for teaching, for reproof, for correction, and for training in righteousness, that the man of God may be complete, equipped for every good work" (2 Timothy 3:16–17). They taught me that God never contradicts himself in the Scriptures, and that I must push through seeming inadequacies, inconsistencies, or contradictions to the fullness of truth. So yes, all my happily meandering Baptist roads and signposts led to serious questions that I had to push through the Protestant veil to answer.

The Holy Spirit led me much the same way he has always led his children, around and around the mountain of his presence. In every revolution, he led me always to new points, new horizons, and then finally to a new realization that the faith I loved and had been nurtured in was simply not enough. There had to be more. Didn't there? Was God so explainable?

I began to experience uneasiness with pat answers and sideways glances at hard questions. I was dissatisfied with the packaged, matter-of-fact way preachers offered the Scriptures to us, as though everything had been explained, and our job, especially as women, was simply to accept the regurgitated half-answers from their wiser hands. I grew disheartened by the suspicion my honest searching aroused, as though my teachers were protecting some secret from my probing. God shook me to the core until my teeth rattled and my religious foundations felt upended at their confrontation with the Church of history.

At first I felt like embracing Catholicism would be a repudiation of all I had known and loved. Rather than a progressive pedagogy, I held the superior view postmodernists do toward anything previous, and the same one many of my non-Catholic brothers and sisters still hold toward the Old Testament: *old* equals "bad, mistaken, outdated, false" and *new* equals "good, right, progressive, and true."

But the Holy Spirit challenged me to follow the lead of Scripture itself, in which Jesus followed and fulfilled rather than denigrated his native Judaism (Matthew 5:17), in which St. Paul praises his Jewish roots (Romans 3:1–2), and the New Testament encourages reverence for and reference to the Old (Matthew 13:52). He retraced the pattern of precept upon precept and line upon line (Isaiah 28:10) with me, wherein righteousness is revealed to us "faith to faith"

(Romans 1:17), each bit building on the last, not knocking it all back down to the ground again to start completely over.

My conversion was never a rejection of the past, then, any more than the New Testament was a rejection or a redo of the Old. If the Old Testament *was* the skeleton for the muscle, sinew, and choreography of the New, then a Protestant immersion in the Scriptures was the muscle memory necessary for my participation in the ballet of ancient Christianity.

Catholicism taught me to grope at the mystery of faith, but one can hardly approach mystery until she has first mastered the basic framework with which to appreciate it. My determined search revealed a whole new world—rich, ancient, mysterious, beckoning. History and Tradition are no dead fossils, then, but the marrow of the Church, which St. Paul says is "the pillar and foundation of truth" (1 Timothy 3:15).

I researched Church history from primary sources rather than non-Catholic narratives of history that turned out to be clearly slanted and selective. That's not to say Protestant bias is *necessarily* purposeful. Unless you're ever exposed to a historical interpretation of some theological issue, Bible verses and books and issues only have certain possible meanings, so everyone propagates the same interpretations until someone begins to wonder at the rote.

I wondered at and questioned the conflicting voices in denominationalism about interpretation of Scripture and history. If it's true that "no Scripture is of private interpretation" (2 Peter 1:20)—a verse I am sure I never clapped eyes on before this time—then there must be a public interpretation, and if so, where is the authoritative public interpretation of Scripture? Shouldn't we know? Wouldn't Jesus take great pains to make sure we know the unequivocal truth about things so foundational and eternally important to man's soul?

He did, and he prepares us for knowing where to find authoritative illumination and truth in the Church from his instruction in the Old Testament tabernacle. At its root, the issue of interpretation of Scripture comes down to God's authority. Scripture is *his* word. No matter what is ever said about it, the right meaning can only be the meaning he intends for it. And in both the Bible and Catholicism, God's authority on earth rests most fully in the priesthood.

TWO TYPES OF PRIESTHOOD

The main problem I had as a Baptist with my Catholic heritage was the institutional priesthood, because everything Catholic (when used as an epithet) seemed to proceed from it. In fact, I have found in my own efforts at evangelization here in the fundamentalist South that nothing irritates people like the priesthood. The priest is usually a person's first direct exposure to Church hierarchy, and let's face it, authority just rubs us all the wrong way when it doesn't conform to what we think or want.

I can say so because my whole spiritual education at God's hands has been on the issue of authority, and it was the number one issue that propelled me into the Church. I emerged from childhood with profound father wounds that provoked sometimes violent rebellion against authority. My dad was aggressive, dominating, and control-ling, so I was determined no one would ever force me to do anything I didn't want, ever again. You can probably imagine how easy and joyful it was to be my father, my husband, my boss. *Ahem*. You can also understand, then, that I had real suspicions about church authority as well, especially given my experiences in denominational churches.

When I was a twenty-something Baptist church leader, there arose a dispute against our pastor. It was nothing more than a personality conflict, really, but I chose a side and had all sorts of opinions that seemed completely righteous and totally just. After all, I could prove every one of those opinions with a Bible verse. The problem was, God contradicted my opinions with his word in lectio divina, and he used the Israelite's rebellion against the priesthood in Numbers 16–17 to do it.

As a Protestant, priesthood seemed harmless enough, because I knew that I, personally, was part of the common, or lay priesthood of God. As St. Peter says, "And like living stones be yourselves built into a spiritual house to be a holy priesthood, to offer spiritual sacrifices acceptable to God through Jesus Christ." (1 Peter 2:5). This idea is sometimes called the "common priesthood" or the "priesthood of the believer."

Interestingly, in the passage above, St. Peter was actually quoting an Old Testament verse from Exodus 19:3–6: "And Moses went up to God, and the Lord called to him out of the mountain, saying, 'Thus you shall say to the house of Jacob, and tell the people of Israel…you shall be to me a kingdom of priests and a holy nation.'" All the people of Israel were to be a kingdom of priests.

I was very familiar with these verses when that church dispute arose, so when I ran across these verses about priesthood in my daily lectio divina at that time, the lay priesthood is the only way I considered those verses to apply beyond the Old Testament. I was too busy complaining about the pastor. Who did he think he was, anyway? We are *all* a "kingdom of priests." But then… I stumbled over something disturbing.

In Numbers 16:1–11, two hundred fifty "leaders, men of renown" rose up against Moses and Aaron in dispute over the authority of Aaron's priesthood, the institutional priesthood, in an attitude very similar to what was happening in my own church: "And they assembled themselves together against Moses and against Aaron, and said to them, 'You have gone too far! For all the congregation are holy, every one of them, and the Lord is among them; why then do you exalt yourselves above the assembly of the Lord?'" (Numbers 16:3).

God had given the people their own role in his service, but they were not satisfied with the common priesthood. The people used God's own words (Exodus 19:6) to justify claiming equal authority and responsibility with the institutional priesthood. Because God had said they were all a kingdom of priests, the people felt the institutional priesthood was unnecessary, a sentiment the vast majority of denominationalism shares.

As I read the account of the dispute, I grew very uneasy about my own complaining, because God ultimately regarded their complaining and rebellion to be against his own authority and leadership. "Therefore it is against the Lord that you and all your company have gathered together" (Numbers 16:11). The institutional priesthood was God's idea, so it was the Lord, himself, they offended by complaining against the priesthood.

Nevertheless, he was happy to clear up the controversy. To satisfy the issue of legitimate authority, God publicly affirmed his institutional priesthood in a remarkable way.

THE RESURRECTION OF THE DEAD STICK

In Numbers 17:1–3, God commanded the leaders of each tribe, all of them shepherds, to give their staffs to Moses to place in his presence in the Holy of Holies. They were basically walking sticks, sometimes called "rods," but were also a sign of tribal authority so that the staff of a tribe leader was the emblem of his tribe or flock. In the Catholic Church, this is the bishop's staff today.

The Holy of Holies in the Tent of the Covenant was where God's presence rested in the cloud. God wanted the staffs brought to him. He would cause the tribal staff, a dead stick, that belonged to the man God had chosen as the father of the priesthood to resurrect and bud with leaves and fruit (Numbers 17:8).

A dead stick one day, and the next day living almond flowers and ripe almonds. God turned Aaron's ordinary shepherd's staff into a final ruling. Then, just to emphasize the point, the Lord commanded the other leaders to receive back their dead staffs from the Holy of Holies in the Tabernacle to show their submission to God's selection. After this episode, God gave the Levite tribe to the Old Testament institutional priesthood as assistants and helpers in the things pertaining to the tabernacle.

This priestly cooperative foreshadows the relationship of our own pope to his brother bishops, and our bishops to their brother priests. Altogether, the Catholic priesthood is the resurrection of the dead stick—through him, with him, in him—of Judaism's obsolete priesthood.

Aaron's rod, living, budded, and fruited with almonds, was to be kept within the ark inside the tabernacle as a continual confirmation to those who would otherwise rebel, that God himself would specially animate this living, fruitful, institutional priesthood. God seems serious about priestly authority! Interestingly, the Hebrew word *almond* comes from the root "to watch." The priesthood would keep watch over the people.

Additionally, by setting up the institutional priesthood as an office, God communicated his desire that it be a perpetual representation of his authority. An office is a position in an organization with specific duties attached to it. The position stays intact while the people who occupy it change. "The priest's office shall be theirs by perpetual statute. Thus you shall ordain them" (Exodus 29:9). This episode in our ancient history serves as a warning that rebellion against the priesthood results in a cycle of bickering, division, and correction.

St. Paul refers to this Old Testament experience when he tells us in Romans 13:1–2, "Let every person be subject to the governing authorities. For there is no authority except from God, and those that exist have been instituted by God. Therefore he who resists the authorities resists what God has appointed, and those who resist will incur judgment."

God used the Old Testament conflict over the priesthood and St. Paul's warning to tell me to keep my mouth shut where my church leaders were concerned. I could talk to him about my complaints. I could even go to the pastor himself, and pursue whatever other options there were in the chain of authority.

But to refuse or resist their authority, to gossip about them, or try to undermine them is a sin. In fact, rebellion was the sin of Satan. But more than that, he used an important function of the authority of the Old Testament priesthood to draw me right into submission to the priestly authority of the historical Church.

CHAIR OF MOSES

Following God's direction given to him on Mount Sinai and confirmed through the budding of Aaron's rod, the great prophet Moses instituted, ordained, and governed the priesthood. As the nation grew, their numbers swelled until other provisions were necessary to accommodate them and assist the priests who carried the responsibility and burden of ministering to them.

For instance, Moses served the people through his calling and authority as the great prophet by applying and rendering judgments from the general principles of God's word in the Law to their specific disputes. Later, this judgment seat came to be known as the Chair of Moses.

But eventually, his father-in-law pointed out that the simultaneous gift and burden of Moses's perfectionism had led to his sitting in judgment all day long every day, and was too overwhelming and time-consuming a practice to continue. Jethro counseled Moses to continue teaching the broad areas of instruction and hearing major matters, but to turn over the more routine, mundane administrative issues and cases to a group of lesser magistrates to help him bear the burden of interpreting and adjudicating for the people (Exodus 18:13–27).

Some believe this group of judges formed the basis for the eventual supreme court of ancient Israel, the Sanhedrin (Numbers 11:16–17). Composed of seventy-one elders, the Sanhedrin was a crucial source of Jewish leadership whose authority was worthy of obedience, according to Jesus (Matthew 23:2). The Sanhedrin was divided even further into a tribunal of twenty-three judges called a Minor Sanhedrin that heard capital crimes.

The Chair of Moses was a phrase used to signify the place of authority that the Scribes and Pharisees occupied in interpreting the Law and exercising authority over the Jewish people. Although they had become corrupt and spiritually dead, Jesus upheld their office of authority as a matter of obedience to God (Matthew 23:1–3). In Greek, the phrase is Moses's *kathedras*, literally "Moses's seat." *Kathedras* is the term from which we get *cathedra*, as in *ex cathedra*, meaning "from the seat" and "cathedral," which is the church in which the seat of the bishop rests, and the final judgment seat of Christ (2 Corinthians 5:10).

Through the tabernacle, God communicated his desire for religious leadership and authority, but not just raw power or control. Proper leadership would ultimately lead God's people into the closest possible relationship with him through particularly special means.

THE LIGHT OF ALMONDS

To the left of the sanctuary entrance in the Old Testament tabernacle, a copy of the temple in heaven, was a piece of equipment used to illuminate it. According to the pattern God gave Moses on Mount Sinai, the base, shaft, branches, bowls, and ornamental knobs and flowers of this instrument were hammered from one gold piece (Exodus. 25:31). From the central stem, its seven branches were beaten out into a golden tree of light. The lampstand was the article in the sanctuary on which the most adornment was lavished, and the light was never allowed to go out (Exodus 27:20–21).

Each branch was topped with a little bowl-lamp containing olive oil and secured with a light-bearing wick. Inside the holy place (the sanctuary) but outside the curtain veiling the ark of testimony in the Holy of Holies, the priests were to maintain the lamps from evening to morning throughout their perpetual generations. The priests kept the wicks trimmed, the oil topped, and the lamps burning before the Lord continuously (Leviticus 24:3–4).

The light from the lampstand would have been reflected in the gold lining the walls of the sanctuary, making the whole room glow. This lampstand is the Jewish menorah, studded all over with ornamental almond flowers that were perpetually symbolic of Aaron's rod and the light-bearing institutional priesthood in the presence of God and emanating his light. The nature of the light radiating from the institutional priesthood becomes clear through further investigation of its trappings.

A POCKETFUL OF SONSHINE

Exodus 28:29–30 describes two unique parts of the institutional priesthood's vestment. The "breastplate of judgment" was a pouch of sorts (literally, a "rational, or pocket"), sewn together on three sides and open at the top under the high priest's chin. This pocket held two mysterious stones, called the Urim and Thummim (Exodus 28:30).

The titles are transliterated, meaning the Hebrew characters are simply changed to corresponding English letters. This is usually done when there is nothing in English to correspond to an ancient word or idea.

These transliterated Hebrew words mean "Lights" and "Perfect Truths," or the "revelation of perfect knowledge," and both are used in the superlative plural (see Sirach 45:10). Together the names mean something similar to "Complete Light" or "Perfect Truth."

The unique stones were used to consult God about his selection of leaders (Numbers 27:21), discernment of guilt or innocence (1 Samuel 14:41), and determination of God's will (Ezra 2:63).

Through these stones, the revelation of God's will was communicated to the Israelites through the High Priest who held the Urim and Thummim stones in the pocket against his breast and was the only persona authorized to use them. Thinking goes that the priest would somehow draw stones in order to determine God's will in a matter, so that the Urim and Thummim together with the priest functioned as the oracle of judgment (Sirach 45:10).

Exactly what the stones looked like or how they were used is unknown, but apparently the high priest phrased direct questions to God in the Holy of Holies so that they could be answered with a simple "yes" or "no," signified by the withdrawing of the corresponding stones from the priest's pocket, or *ephod*. This is why it was stored in the "breastplate of judgment."

Because the Urim and Thummim were used to communicate God's word and will, the Church Fathers understood the "Lights and Truths" to mean the light of doctrine.

Similarly, part of the duty of the priesthood was to instruct and teach the people about the Law (Deuteronomy. 33:8) so that between the Ten Commandments, the Torah, and the Urim and Thummim, the people would have comprehensive, authoritative judgments and teachings they could trust, teachings the Scriptures repeatedly call "light."

The priest, then, is called the "prince of the sanctuary" (Sirach 45:30, DRB), and the Scriptures offer a soaring description of the functions of the priesthood and list that their duties are to bless, to offer sacrifice, and to *teach and apply the law* (Sirach 45:15–17, emphasis added). "For the lips of a priest should guard knowledge, and men should seek instruction from his mouth, for he is the messenger of the Lord of hosts" (Malachi 2:7).

Priesthood in the Church

Perfection is the end of every divine arrangement, yet the Old Testament system could not bring it about (Hebrews 7:11). Therefore, the institutional priesthood had to be changed (Hebrews 7:12), not eliminated, for that would contradict God's command that it remain forever, but literally "exchanged" (Hebrews 7:12).

The Old Testament institutional priesthood is a type of New Testament institutional priesthood in Christ. The New Testament priesthood is not through physical progeny, as was the Old Testament Aaronic priesthood, but through Christ's selection and spiritual progeny as his ordination of the apostles illustrates. The Old Law, facilitated for the people by the priesthood, could not bring people to perfection (maturity or holiness); it could not bring us to God (Hebrews 7:18–19).

The Law brought nothing to perfection, for of itself it communicated no sanctifying grace and gave no power to do the good which it commanded. The introduction of grace through Christ is what makes the new covenant and new priesthood in him better. The term "better" is used ten times in the book of Hebrews to describe the new covenant. The grace conferred through the sacramental system of the New Testament priesthood in Christ *can* bring about complete salvation and perfection, and bring us "near to God" (Hebrews 7:19). "It is not the Old Testament that is abolished in Christ but the concealing veil, so that it may be understood through Christ."[1] Jesus, himself the Urim and Thummim of "perfect truth" and the Light of the World (John 8:12), fulfills this institutional priestly office and brings it forward into the New Testament Church so that it remains perpetual as God commanded, as we see beautifully illustrated in the book of Revelation.

Jesus Our High Priest

Possibly one of the most thrilling visions of heaven for me (Sonja) is in the book of Revelation. Part of the apocalyptic genre (*apocalypse*, meaning "revelation"), the subject of which is end times prophecy, Revelation is full of symbolic images and numbers. Its grotesque monsters, angels, creatures, and sinners in the throes of punishment are characteristic of this genre, all literary "props" laden with symbolic meaning that form the surrealistic feel and landscape of the narrative.

The opening salvo is St. John's vision of heaven, and what he sees is Jesus, the Light of the World (John 8:12), standing in the middle of seven golden menorahs, each menorah seven-branched and covered in gold almond blossoms. He is wearing priestly vestments, his word proceeds from his mouth like a sword, and he holds seven stars that are said to be the priests of the seven churches (Revelation 1:12–20). These pastors and churches were actually in existence at the time John wrote Revelation, but many believe they are also symbolic of the eras of the earthly Church. Either way, Jesus stands in the midst of the institutional priesthood as the light of the world, administrating and illuminating them with the light of doctrine, so they illuminate all of the New Testament Church and history.

St. John saw Jesus the high priest in the eternity of heaven. The New Testament book of Hebrews was written to Jews, in part, to explain the fulfillment of the old covenant priesthood and Law in Jesus as the new Moses and our new, eternal High Priest of the new covenant. "Therefore, holy brethren, who share in a heavenly call, consider Jesus, the apostle and high priest of our confession" (Hebrews 3:1–6).

Just as the seven lampstands surrounding Jesus in the heavenly temple (Revelation 1:12–13) depict Jesus at the center of the institutional, Catholic priesthood, the same seven lampstands radiating outwardly from the light of the world depict the whole of the historical Church, led by the episcopacy, as the sacred illumination of the world. They occupy the priestly office through him, in him, and with him, as is indicated in the continuation of Judas's institutional office as priestly apostle after his suicide (Acts 1:20), and they are led by the Rock (1 Corinthians 10:4) through the rock.

CHAIR OF THE ROCK

Jesus, referring to the prophet Isaiah, pronounced the Jewish priest-hood dead as "whitewashed sepulchers" (Isaiah 22:16; Matthew 23:27). As prophesied, Jesus overthrew their leadership and resurrected the dead stick of their priesthood by calling a new leader of a new priesthood for his universal Church.

To him he gave the keys of administrative and governing responsibilities for his house,[2] established him on a glorious seat (throne or chair) from which he would adjudicate (open and shut), and made him a father to his people (*pope*, meaning "papa"): "You are Peter [meaning "rock"] and upon this rock I will build my church." (Isaiah 22:15–25; Matthew 16:17–19, emphasis ours). The Church of history fulfills Isaiah's prophecy and upholds the office of Peter's chair.[3]

> The Lord says to Peter: "I say to you," He says, "that you are Peter, and upon this rock I will build my Church, and the gates of hell will not overcome it. And to you I will give the keys of the kingdom of heaven: and whatever things you bind on earth shall be bound also in heaven, and whatever you loose on earth, they shall be loosed also in heaven." And again he says to him after his resurrection: "Feed my sheep." On him he builds the Church, and to him he gives the command to feed the sheep; and although he assigns a like power to all the Apostles, yet he founded a single chair, and he established by his own authority a source and an intrinsic reason for that unity.
>
> Indeed, the others were that also which Peter was; but a primacy is given to Peter, whereby it is made clear that there is but one Church and one chair. So too, all are shepherds, and the flock is shown to be one, fed by all the Apostles in single-minded accord. If someone does not hold fast to this unity of Peter, can he imagine that he still holds the faith? If he desert

the chair of Peter upon whom the Church was built, can he still be confident that he is in the Church?"[4]

Magisterial "Menorah"

Like Moses, his priesthood and elders, and the Jewish Sanhedrin after them, the Church is watched over and illuminated by the ministry of the priestly and apostolic magisterium. The Deposit of Faith, which includes the Bible and sacred Tradition, has been guarded and preserved for us for two millennia by the teaching authority of the Church (see CCC, 84 and 85).

Magisterium is a Latin term meaning "teaching office." Our magisterium governs through the papacy or chair of Peter, Church councils and documents as in Acts 15, and various synods of bishops. Working in unity with each other in Christ as the heavenly lampstands in Revelation indicate, the magisteria are the official interpreters of sacred Scripture (writings) and sacred Tradition (oral teachings), sometimes called "the golden chain," both of them equally authoritative as oracles of God.

As St. Paul commands, we need both Scripture and Tradition: "So then, brethren, stand firm and hold to the traditions which you were taught by us, either by word of mouth [Tradition] or by letter [Scripture]" (2 Timothy 2:15). The Church, and indeed all of mankind, needs this light and truth. "There is an organic connection between our spiritual life and the dogmas. Dogmas are lights along the path of faith; they illuminate it and make it secure. Conversely, if our life is upright, our intellect and heart will be open to welcome the light shed by the dogmas of faith" (*CCC,* 89).

God halted the cycle of divisions among the Israelites in the Old Testament through his confirmation of the priesthood's authority as his own. The primary reason there are in excess of twenty-five thousand non-Catholic denominations and innumerable conflicting interpretations of the Scriptures is the great lack of central, authoritative leadership. "The Bible is self-interpreting," they say. "The Holy Spirit and me." If the Bible really had complete self-interpreting capacity, would not 100 percent of the people who read it come to the same exact interpretations, 100 percent of the time? There would be no divisions.

St. Paul reminds us God is "not a god of confusion but of peace" (1 Corinthians 14:33) and forbids divisions (1 Corinthians. 1:12), because there is only one Lord, one faith, and one baptism (Ephesians 4:5).

Jesus gave the power to bind and loose to the apostles and their successors, the holy order of bishops led by Peter, not just in the forgiveness of sins but in all things pertaining to faith and morals: "*Whatever* you bind on earth will be bound in heaven, and whatever you loose on earth will be loosed in heaven" (Matthew 18:18, emphasis ours). Five chapters later (Matthew 23:2–3), Jesus clearly exhorted his followers to adhere to those in the office and the chair: "The scribes and the Pharisees have taken their seat on the chair of Moses. Therefore, *do and observe all things whatsoever they tell you*" (emphasis ours).

Following Jesus as our new Moses, the new chair is the See (seat) of Peter, which Jesus established, along with the college of his brother bishops who enjoy the fullness of the priesthood of Jesus Christ. All priests have the power to consecrate the sacred elements at Mass, whereby bread and wine become the sacrificial Body and Blood of Jesus by the power of the Holy Spirit. Bishops have this same power and authority, and additionally the power to ordain new priests for the sake of the Eucharist.

The role of the bishop (*episcopae*) is that of "the new high priest," established by God himself in the Old Testament and "in the language of the Fathers of the Church...is the supreme power of the sacred ministry."[5] This important document of Vatican II also articulates the historical Church's understanding that bishops hold the title of Vicar of Christ.[6]

The mission of the bishop shepherds is, therefore, "To be with God through Christ's mediation and, as Christ's emissary, to bring God to men—this is the mission of the bishop. 'He who does not gather with me scatters' says Jesus (Matthew 12:30): the bishop's raison d'être is to gather with Jesus."[7]

Magisterial Music

Two friends were driving home from a golf outing. While listening to the radio in the car, a beautiful piano etude by Frederic Chopin began to play. The two men were so moved by the beauty of the music, that they decided right then and there to learn how to play piano. They decided to get together one year from that day and celebrate their achievement by playing the same piano etude they heard on the radio.

When they arrived home, the first friend said to himself, "I'm a pretty smart guy. I don't need anyone to teach me how to play piano; I can figure it out all on my own." So he went to the local music store, bought a how-to-play-piano book, and proceeded to teach himself how to play. However, the business of everyday life—phone calls, text messages, email, and social media, and socializing with friends—frequently distracted him. He continued in this same pattern for the next year.

Meanwhile, his golfing buddy, also intelligent, assessed his situation and determined that he was clueless about playing piano. He decided to hire a teacher. The teacher helped him discover the basic principles and skills involved in playing piano: how to read music, body positioning, what the black and white keys do, musical theory and history, all of it. Over time, he learned scales, modes, and harmony. He practiced an hour a day. He often didn't feel like practicing but because he made a commitment, he decided to stay with it and maintained the discipline of practicing every day. He continued this pattern for the next year.

Exactly one year later, both friends got together to play the piano etude. The first friend began to play but became frustrated and discouraged because the music he heard in his head could not be expressed fully on the piano. Meanwhile, the second friend was not only playing the notes of the song skillfully and accurately, he was also able to joyfully and passionately express himself through the music.

Both friends, moved by beauty, truly desired to play piano; to be able to express themselves through the beauty they encountered. Both used their free will to say, "I want to do this" but the first friend tried to learn on his own—the way he felt like doing it—making a conscious decision not to follow the objective rules of piano playing. Ultimately, he was frustrated and miserable because he became a slave to his passions, succumbing to sloppy subjective truth that led to his being musically unhappy and unfulfilled.

Conversely, the second friend used his free will to align himself with the transcendent rules and principles of playing piano. He developed good habits and customs that took long hours of practice to perfect.

The same is true for us when we follow the teachings of the Church in faith and morals. The Church is the piano teacher, the divine pedagogue, who gives us the principles of how to live our faith in accord with the teachings of Jesus Christ. Living virtuously takes long hours of practice, but it is through this discipline that we become the person that God created and calls us to be.

We want to express individuality and uniqueness, and we find out quickly that true uniqueness is only truly expressed when rooted in a solid foundation of transcendent principles. This is why we can hear twenty different piano virtuosos play the exact same piece of music and each sounds different—their uniqueness and individuality shines through in their playing. The common factor is that they all started out agreeing to totally master the objective principles that control how music works. Only on a foundation of transcendent principles could they develop genuine distinctiveness. In other words, in order to have true uniqueness and individuality you have to root yourself in something that is true, good, and beautiful.

The Church teaches that by freely submitting ourselves to God's law and to his loving care and protection, we experience abundant life as God's children more and more fully. God allows his sons and daughters to participate in his creative, life-giving work.

This is the Father's gift to us: to allow us to love as he loves, to give ourselves to him fully, completely, and freely just as Christ poured out his love for us fully, completely, and freely on the cross. This is why faithfully living out of the Church's teachings, especially in the area of conscience and the moral life, bear tremendous fruits for those who are willing to follow God's law with all their heart, soul, mind and strength. The great saint and Doctor of the Church, St. Augustine, summarizes this idea beautifully: "Our hearts are restless until they rest in Thee."

The Chair of Peter and the magisterium of the Church constitute this beautiful, priceless golden chain of religious authority and the proper interpretation of the Scriptures. What the Church says about a matter of faith and morals is what God says about it. We must read and study the Bible with the mind of the Church if we are to be illumined with the fullness of the light of truth in Christ.

Let's Review
- *"Public interpretation" means that when we read and study Scripture, we must do so within the living Tradition* of the whole historical Church.
- *All of us in the Church—past, present, and future—are under "one Lord, one faith, one baptism" (Ephesians 4:5).*

- *The Bible is the most mysterious and difficult book ever written* and ever published.
- *We must approach our study of the Bible with a respect for the Christians of history*, especially those who lived, wrote, and were martyred closest to the apostles, and indeed were directly taught and ordained by them.
- *Our ancient Tradition is a rich source of teaching*, knowledge, and blessing that helps protect us from error and teaches us to live beautifully.
- *The Catholic magisterium is the voice of the Holy Spirit* in interpretation of Scripture.

INVITATION

The most painful period of my (Sonja) life involved difficulty in understanding authority properly. The more of the fullness of truth I discovered in the Church, the more difficult my position in denominationalism became for me, as a woman and wife. Friends of mine quoted "Wives obey your husbands" to me as proof that I was stepping out from under God's authority through my husband by exploring and embracing the truth I was learning. "All authority is given by God" was quoted to deter me from any further research apart from my denominational tradition.

In my daily lectio divina, I read, "Whoever knows what is right to do and fails to do it, for him it is sin" (James 4:17). I was sinning by searching for the truth apart from my leaders (naysayers said), and I was sinning by not following the truth I found in the Catholic Church. What's a girl to do?

I looked to Mary, who said "yes" to God apart from Joseph or her family or Judaism, but without flaunting or dividing or rebelling or inciting. She simply allowed God to do something in her. In doing so, he defended and affirmed her. God will always make your vindication dawn like the sun in response to this type of deep humility (Isaiah 62:1).

When we must dissent, and sometimes it is a matter of sin not to, we must do the right thing and leave all the consequences to God as Mary did.

God Prompt—LOVE the Word

Lectio—Listen

When…Mary had been betrothed to Joseph, before they came together she was found to be with child of the Holy Spirit; and her husband Joseph, being a just man and unwilling to put her to shame, resolved to divorce her quietly.

But as he considered this, behold, an angel of the Lord appeared to him in a dream, saying, 'Joseph, son of David, do not fear to take Mary your wife, for that which is conceived in her is of the Holy Spirit; she will bear a son, and you shall call his name Jesus, for he will save his people from their sins.'

…When Joseph woke from sleep, he did as the angel of the Lord commanded him (Matthew 1:18–24).

Oratio—Observe

Do you wonder how long Mary waited on God to send Joseph the dream that confirmed her purity? How hard was it for her to refrain from defending herself in the community while praying God would do it for her? While waiting for him to decide, did she pack up and tell Joseph it was time to go to Egypt while mounting the donkey and "letting" him walk? Did she complain when he took her to a barn to give birth to the Savior of the world? Did she murmur as she watched her Son falsely accused? Did she speak out on her own or his behalf?

What was it like to be assumed into heaven and crowned queen?

Is it because Mary is so submissive to God that she is so powerful?

Meditatio—Verbalize

Lord, as I consider my relationship to authority I feel…

Lord, I am most often tempted to rebel against your authority when…

Lord, help me to be fully alive to your holy presence, speaking and moving through those in authority over me. Enfold me in your love. Let my will become one with yours.

Contemplatio—Entrust
Right now, just be in the Lord's presence and allow your heart to respond to his love.

chapter ten

The Word Is a Person

Jesus came into the world in a specific geographical, historical, and theological context. More simply, he came and lived in Palestine, at the climax of centuries of Jewish history, within the framework of a progressive revelation that was permanently recorded in the Bible. Since an understanding of the setting within which God offers him to us is essential to apprehending Jesus as fully as possible, we have explored this context and framework as the springboard for further investigation. Where do we go from here?

In moving forward, we are clear that we should always approach the Bible as God's word to us. Because it is the inspired, inerrant (meaning without error) revelation of Jesus Christ, the Bible is often called the Word of God. But the Word of God is a person, not a book.

"In the beginning," it is said, "was the Word, and the Word was with God, and the Word was God" (John 1:1). The Word of God is a person, Jesus Christ. Jesus is the final revelation and expression, or "speech," of God (Hebrews 1:1–4).[1] A person cannot be contained in a book, as St. John expresses, "But there are also many other things which Jesus did; were every one of them to be written, I suppose that the world itself could not contain the books that would be written" (John 21:25).

Human language has a certain limitation and tension, so the Word of God is incarnate in the person of Jesus precisely because they are human words and, therefore, necessarily inhibit a complete communication of him, as the *Catechism* tells us.

Through all the words of Sacred Scripture, God speaks only one single Word, his one Utterance in whom he expresses himself completely:

You recall that one and the same Word of God extends throughout Scripture, that it is one and the same Utterance that resounds in the mouths of all the sacred writers, since he who was in the beginning God with God has no need of separate syllables; for he is not subject to time.

For this reason, the Church has always venerated the Scriptures as she venerates the Lord's Body. She never ceases to present to the faithful the bread of life, taken from the one table of God's Word and Christ's Body.

In Sacred Scripture, the Church constantly finds her nourishment and her strength, for she welcomes it not as a human word, 'but as what it really is, the word of God'. In the sacred books, the Father who is in heaven comes lovingly to meet his children, and talks with them (*CCC*, 102–104).

THE LIMITATION OF WORDS

Divine revelation as the fullness of the deposit of faith, then, is handed on to us through the Scriptures *and* Tradition[2] (from the Latin *traditio*, meaning "to hand on or over"), just as St. Paul upholds: "So then, brethren, stand firm and hold to the traditions which you were taught by us, either by word of mouth or by letter" (2 Thessalonians 2:15).

Together, they are "like a mirror in which the pilgrim Church on earth looks at God, from whom she has received everything, until she is brought finally to see him as he is, face to face" (see 1 John 3:2).[3] Whenever we read and study the Bible with the mind and heart of the Church, we are deepening our relationship with the person of Christ, of whom all the Scriptures and history testify (Revelation 19:10).

The Old Testament was the body of Scriptures for the first generation of Christians. They did not yet have a written New Testament, and the New Testament itself demonstrates the process of living Tradition. Before there was ever a single writing about Jesus, the early Christians followed something else.

The book of Acts tells us about the birthday of the Church, in which we learn that the early Church followed something called "The Way" for authoritative Christian teaching and practice. Because there was no such thing, yet, as a Bible, the early Church communicated Jesus's teachings through this binding oral Tradition that they called "The Way." In fact, conforming to this Way was one of three requirements a writing had to meet in order to be considered part of the eventual, official collection of sacred Scripture—*Scriptures* meaning "writings."

We see then that Tradition predates Scripture (both Old Testament and New Testament) and is responsible for the canon; Scripture itself is an expression of Tradition.

A Library of Love

In our day and time, we commonly think of the Bible as a single book, but it's actually a small library of books. The word bible comes from the Greek word *biblia*, meaning "books." We capitalize the word Bible in order to emphasize the sacredness of its books.

Each book was originally a single scroll. Old Testament Hebrew is read right to left, while the New Testament was written in all capital Greek letters with no spaces or punctuation. The original scrolls had no chapter or verse designations. One ancient manuscript contains the end of Luke and beginning of John on the same page. What a gift our convenient one-volume set, translations, separations, labels, and headings are!

All the scrolls were eventually selected as authoritative, collected, and bound, but not until the fourth century AD. The selection of books that is considered part of Scripture is called the "canon," meaning "measuring stick." Jewish rabbis selected the Old Testament canon. The apostles used a Greek translation of the Old Testament called the Septuagint in their preaching and teaching. Through their writings, writings that comprise most of the New Testament, we know something of what they considered authoritative by the body of quotes they used from the Septuagint. The Septuagint that they used included all of the books in our Catholic Bibles.

The New Testament canon was decided by determining if the writing was of the Way, the oral Tradition of the apostles; if it was written by an apostle or was apostolic; and by whether or not it was circulated throughout the churches from the beginning. The Catholic Church selected and determined the New Testament canon.

Around 1500 Martin Luther and those who followed him removed several books from the canon, so non-Catholic Bibles are missing several books. Scripture includes the full canon of sacred books in both the Old and New Testaments, and Tradition includes Church doctrine, life, and worship that serves to help the Church live holy lives and increase our faith. Like two halves of a single nut, apostolic Tradition and sacred Scripture together compose the one deposit of faith.

Big T and Little t Are Four D's

There are many non-binding disciplinary, liturgical (meaning *ceremonial*), and/or devotional traditions that arose in the local churches over time. Those are "small t" traditions that can and often do change with time or circumstance. "Big T" Tradition is distinguished from various theological, disciplinary, liturgical, or devotional traditions, born in the local churches over time. In the light of Tradition, these traditions can be retained, modified, or even abandoned under the guidance of the Church's magisterium. But sacred Tradition is part of the deposit of faith preserved for us by the Church throughout two millennia. Because Tradition is the word of God, it is authoritative, and we capitalize the word.

Other written expressions of Tradition are the writings of the Fathers and doctors, papal encyclicals, and council writings, but they are not referred to as "inspired" or called "the Word of God." They fall into the "Four D's": *Dogma* are truths proposed by the Church as being part of or necessarily connected to Revelation in a binding, definitive way, which comprise the unchangeable part of the deposit of faith (the Holy Eucharist, for example); *Doctrine* is what the Church believes, teaches, and confesses on the authority of the Word of God (Jesus Christ), the understanding of which can develop over time but never change (the structure of the Mass and teachings in the documents of Vatican II, for example); *Disciplines*, which are widely practiced but changeable (as in meatless Fridays and priestly celibacy); and *Devotions*, which are often a matter of personal preference or matter of duty and station in life (as in a daily rosary). Doctrines, disciplines, and devotions are part of the growth in insight into the realities and words being passed on.[4] As the Holy Spirit guides the Church "into all truth" (John 16:13), she "penetrates it more deeply, applies it more."[5]

Jesus Christ entrusted the authentic interpretation of Scripture and Tradition to the living teaching office of the Church alone, the magisterium, whose authority is exercised in Christ's name. Ultimately, there is only one source of Revelation, the person of Christ, which has two expressions, Tradition and sacred Scripture. Both are directed at the life of the Church. Together sacred Scripture and Tradition convey the Word of God.[6] Apart from the living teaching authority of the Catholic Church, we are easily led into serious mistakes and error by the enemy.

Because Tradition goes back to when the Bible was written, we know what the Bible was and was not meant to communicate to us. Because the Holy Spirit "guides us into all truth" (John 16:13) through the teaching authority Jesus gave his apostles and which they handed down through the Church, the Church's teachings on faith and morals is infallible (Matthew 18:18).

The word of God is inspired, meaning "God-breathed" (2 Timothy 3:16). The Bible is sacred literature because God is the author. He inspired and guided its writing through various human authors, but the Bible is God telling his own story. Because God continues to speak to us through it, "the word of God is living and active, sharper than any two-edged sword, piercing to the division of soul and spirit, of joints and marrow, and discerns the thoughts and intentions of the heart" (Hebrews 4:12). So sacred Scripture remains the primary written expression of Tradition. Through both written and oral Tradition, God invites us to share his life.

Once we are comfortable with daily lectio divina and are ready to embark on deeper study, it is essential to keep this maxim to heart, and always study with the mind of the Church so we are not misled by persuasive, but incomplete and even erroneous interpretations. How do we know what the golden chain of Tradition says about a passage? How do we avoid the interpretative confusion we encounter throughout Christendom? There are many wonderful ways!

Senses of Scripture

In chapter three, we explored an essential principle in Bible study: that the Bible is ancient literature, and uses ancient literary genres and techniques to communicate its message of salvation. In studying the Bible, we have to keep in mind how these forms and techniques work, or the message intended by the original authors will be lost on us.

Often passages in the Bible (especially in the Old Testament) appear confusing because we are trying to read it with a twenty-first-century mindset without recognizing how someone within the time period would have understood what was being said. Let us imagine, for example, that we are in the year 2101.

A group of archeologists is digging at a recently discovered twentieth-century actor's theatre in San Francisco that was destroyed by an earthquake in 1989. Buried in the rubble, they find a VHS tape. The very excited scientists carefully excavate the tape and bring it to a nearby museum that has a working VCR player. After painstakingly repairing and restoring as much of the tape as they could, the archeologists load the VHS tape into the machine and push "Play." The tape is grainy and somewhat choppy, but they are able to decipher some of the content. It reveals a conversation between two actors.

One of the actors is heard saying to the other, "Get out there and break a leg!" The scientists are horrified. One of them writes an article about the VHS artifact, stating that the tape clearly reveals that twentieth-century people were barbarians.

The above example illustrates the importance of literary form, genre, syntax, and so on, when attempting to read and understand sacred Scripture. Like the archeologists who viewed the VHS tape with a twenty-second-century mindset, thereby not appreciating the fact that the twentieth-century colloquial expression "break a leg" actually means "good luck," those who read Scripture without understanding the proper literary and historical context (which leads to the deeper, spiritual meaning) will not understand and, consequently, misinterpret what they are reading. This is why the Catholic Church has a "both-and" approach to understanding and interpreting the Bible, known as the "senses" of Scripture.

After reading with the mind of the Church, the intent, what the sacred writers meant to express under the guidance of the Holy Spirit, is the first and most important rule in deeper study. It is called the *literal sense*. The literal sense of a passage can and often does include metaphors and symbols (think apocalyptic books, as in Revelation) that the original audience would have recognized right away, but that are difficult for us, millennia removed from the writing. So the literal sense is not necessarily the same as literalism, and when studying the Bible for meaning, we need to understand when the author is speaking symbolically or metaphorically.

After the literal sense, the *spiritual senses* are where we seek to discover what the divine author intends to say through the Bible. The first, called the *allegorical sense*, allows us to acquire a more profound understanding of biblical events by recognizing their significance in light of Jesus Christ. The crossing of the Red Sea in Exodus 14, for example, where the Israelites escaped from slavery in Egypt, is seen allegorically as a precursor to baptism where, by his death and resurrection, Jesus frees us from slavery to sin and death.

The second spiritual sense, called the tropological or *moral sense*, points out how we ought to live and act justly. The Ten Commandments in the Old Testament (see Exodus 20 and Deuteronomy 5) and the Beatitudes in the New Testament (see Matthew 5) would be examples of the moral sense of Scripture.

The third, called the *anagogical sense*, views realities and events in the Bible in terms of their eternal significance, leading us upward toward our true Promised Land, the heavenly Jerusalem. These passages in Scripture foreshadow what heaven is like. Jesus, for example, compares our experience in heaven to a wedding feast (see Matthew 22 and Revelation 19).

Knowing the senses of Scripture and why they are important is critical to a proper Catholic understanding of the Bible. But "all other senses of Sacred Scripture are based on the literal,"[7] so the spiritual senses of a passage must always remain secondary to the literal sense. The senses are fluid and dynamic since the full meaning of Scripture is itself inexhaustible. God's story is also our story. The better we know Scripture, the more we can see ourselves on every page. Here's how *we* do it.

Deacon Harold's Study Tools and Habits

My study tools and habits are intimately connected to my diaconal ministry and my speaking apostolate. These include:

Lectio Divina. I learned to love this during my time with the Benedictines. I often use lectio when writing my homilies as a way of connecting God's Word in the Sunday liturgy to the everyday lived experience of the faithful. When we come together as God's family at the Holy Sacrifice of the Mass, we should not sit back like mere spectators while the readings pass us by because our minds are someplace else. We need to walk more closely with Jesus on the road to Emmaus. When the word of God is proclaimed, we should praise God and exclaim with joy, "Did our hearts not burn within us when he opened the Scriptures to us?" (Luke 24:32). Lectio helps me to recapture a sense of awe and wonder in listening to and appreciating the depth of God's word in the Mass (see Nehemiah 8:8–10).

This Spirit-filled joy can only come from God's Word, which is not just pages in a book, but a person—our Lord Jesus Christ! St. John in his Gospel says that "in the beginning was the Word, and the Word was with God, and the Word was God. […] And the Word became flesh and dwelt among us, full of grace and truth" (John 1:1; 14). In lectio divina, we don't just read about Jesus; we encounter him. We don't just become friends with Jesus; we fall in love with him. We don't simply say we are good people; we give our lives to him. Lectio has allowed me to see the story of my life in the pages of the Bible and connects me more deeply and intimately to Christ himself.

Liturgy of the Hours. When I was ordained as a deacon, I took a vow to pray the Liturgy of the Hours (also called the Divine Office) every day on behalf of the Church. The bulk of the Office are the Old Testament Psalms. I can honestly say there has not been a feeling, emotion, or experience that I have not encountered in the Psalms.

My approach to praying the psalms is summed up beautifully by the late Thomas Merton:

> In the Psalms, we drink divine praise at its pure and stainless source in all its sincerity and perfection. The Psalms are not only the songs of prophets inspired by God, they are the songs of the whole Church, the very expression of her deepest inner life....
>
> God has given Himself to her in them, as though in a sacrament. In them, she is singing of her knowledge of God, of her union with Him. The tremendous impact of the Psalms is buried at a very deep spiritual level, and we must pray on that level in order to feel it at all.... There is one fundamental religious experience which the Psalms can all teach us: the peace that comes from submission to God's will and from perfect confidence in Him.
>
> It is by singing the Psalms, by meditating on them, loving them, using them in all the incidents of our spiritual life, that we enable ourselves to enter more deeply into that active participation in the liturgy which is the key to the deepest and truest interior life.[8]

Eucharistic Adoration. Mother Teresa of Calcutta once said, "We cannot separate our lives from the Eucharist.... Jesus has made Himself the Bread of Life to give us life. Night and day, he is there. If you really want to grow in love, come back to the Eucharist, come back to that Adoration."[9]

The reality of Christ's presence in the Eucharist, as Mother Teresa so beautifully reminds us, is at the heart and soul of what it means to be Catholic. The Eucharist is the principal source of strength and nourishment for our souls precisely because it is Christ himself whom we receive. The power of the Eucharistic Christ—present at the Holy Sacrifice of the Mass and in Adoration—gives us the perseverance and fortitude to stand up to the convictions and truths of our faith: to be the disciples that Christ calls us to be. Adoration helps me to hear God.

How do we hear God? Yes, we listen to the readings and read Scripture, but when do we actually hear God? We listen to the Word with our ears but in order to truly hear him we must take St. Benedict's advice: "Listen to the Master's precepts and incline the ear of your heart." The heart is the starting place of hearing the Word of God and observing it.

The key to listening with your heart is silence. The noise and distractions of the culture do not speak to the ear of the heart.

The Scriptures cry out to us, "Truly I have set my soul in silence and peace" (Psalm 131:2), and again, "Indeed, you love truth in the heart, then in the secret of my heart teach me wisdom" (Psalm 51:8), and once more, "Be still and know that I am God" (Psalm 46:11).

Every major decision in my life—from joining the monastery, to getting married, to leaving my job to work full-time in my apostolate, to editing this book—were all made before the Lord in Adoration. We must foster an atmosphere of prayerful silence in order to hear the Word of God and allow that voice to change our lives.

Academic Journals. This feeds the nerdy part of me. I rarely watch television, and spend most of my time reading about and studying the Catholic faith. I subscribe to several theological journals and read them on the plane. I particularly like rooting what I'm reading in the Scriptures.

For example, I recently read an article on the Trinity, and reflected on how men and women reflect the image and likeness of God in Genesis 1. Both men and women are called upon to image God, but, as St. John Paul II taught that "women are more capable than men of paying attention to another person, and that…the man—even though he shares in the parenting relationship—always remains 'outside' the process of pregnancy and the baby's birth; in many ways he has to learn his own 'fatherhood' from the mother."[10]

The woman, in her way of embodying the likeness of God, points to God's immanence and "withinness" since motherhood involves a special communion with the mystery of life as it develops in the woman's womb. In general, a woman's identity is more interiorly focused, intimately linked to her being and "bodiliness" that points to God's heart—the perichoresis of the divine persons in the intimate exchange of love and life between the Father, Son, and Holy Spirit.

The man, in his way of embodying the image of God, points to God's otherness and transcendence, where a man's identity, in general, is more exteriorly focused and closely associated with his actions—with the realization of himself in relation to the external world. Thinking and reflecting on the Scriptures at this level helps me to see more deeply into God's heart.

Biblical History Books. I always get a better sense of the Scriptures when I know about the people, language, and culture that surrounds the Biblical texts. This helps me to root the Scriptures within the context of the time and place in which God's people lived, worked, and prayed.

Knowing the history and how society functioned at the time of Jesus helps make the Gospel's message clearer. For example, in the parable of the Good Samaritan, why did the priest and Levite not assist the man who had been assaulted? Why did Jesus choose the route between Jerusalem and Jericho as the setting for this story? Historical books on Jewish custom and culture provide the answers.

In addition, extra-biblical and secular writers (many hostile to Christianity) point to numerous details of time, dates, people and places in Roman antiquity that corroborate the details in the Gospels, including the Roman writings of Tacitus, Suetonius, Thallus, and

Pliny the Younger, and the Jewish writings of Josephus and the Talmud. One scholar has cited a total of thirty-nine ancient extra-biblical sources, including seventeen non-Christian, that witness from outside the New Testament to over one hundred details of Jesus's life, death, and resurrection.

Bible Commentaries. Like biblical history books, commentaries are very helpful in providing background information, historical perspective, cultural context, units of measure, concordance functions, and many other helpful tools that will encourage you to roll up your sleeves and dive in to knowing God more personally and intimately in the Bible.

I recommend the following: *Ignatius Catholic Study Bible—New Testament* (Ignatius Press), *The Catholic Commentary on Holy Scripture* (1953 edition), all volumes of the *Catholic Commentary in Sacred Scripture* (Baker Books), *The Navarre Bible Commentary*, the *JPS Torah Commentary* (Jewish Publication Society), and *The Jewish Annotated New Testament: New Revised Standard Version* (Oxford University Press).

Interlinear Bible. This resource will help you make sense of the original languages used in the Bible (Hebrew, Greek, and Aramaic) without being a Scripture scholar. Knowing what the words actually mean has been a tremendous source of blessing to me on my journey to connect more deeply with God's word.

For example, Psalm 111:10 says, "The fear of the LORD is the beginning of wisdom; a good understanding have all those who practice it." Examining this verse out of context, the reader assumes that he needs to be afraid of God in order to show he has wisdom. This interpretation would contradict the God of love who created us in his image and likeness. The word for "fear" (*yare* in Hebrew) also means "honor, reverence and respect." This is the proper context for understanding why we must fear God. This is the attitude that children show to their father, and the God of the universe is truly our Father in heaven.

Sonja's Study Tools and Habits

Like Deacon Harold, my lectio and study tools and habits are intimately connected to my ministry and apostolate. My study habits are a bit unruly, because at any given time I am studying and preparing for several different outlets: a radio show topic,[11] a local classroom topic, a speaking talk, a book topic.

As a Third Order Carmelite in formation, I approach all serious Bible study as prayer too, so lectio and analysis-type study are so much a part of my life that they aren't even discernable from each other anymore. I am frequently guilty of beginning to study a particular book or passage, and look up to find I have spent hours following rabbit trails of one Bible or Catechism reference after another and learning piles of Bible trivia, or that my curiosity has led me to some transformative truth I was not looking for at all! In saying that, I encourage you to follow your interests.

For instance, if as you are reading Genesis 3 you wonder why the serpent approached Eve first, rather than Adam, stop reading. Consult your commentaries. Read the notes in your study Bible(s). Read the passage in several different translations.[12] Look up major words and ideas in a Catholic Bible dictionary, and go deeper with the Catholic Encyclopedia.[13] If you don't get clarity, ask God for the answer, and continue to meditate on the passage throughout the day or days to come.

Perhaps as you are mowing the lawn or folding laundry, you experience a flash of insight. Maybe you consider that Eve was more vulnerable—or rather more powerful somehow, instead!—and Satan came against her for it as the serpent. Maybe you will pause with your hand on that zero-turn handle bar or over that pair of miniature Batman underwear and ask God to make you more conscious of temptation. See? Lawn and laundry duties can be good things!

Whenever you ask God for an increase in some virtue, like awareness of temptations, always watch out for what I call pop quizzes.[14]
In our Genesis example, you would anticipate an overt temptation in
the near future. That is the Holy Spirit using your real-life circumstances as an opportunity to practice what you are learning.

Mostly that's my lectio-with-study practice. I also like to study
topics: fear, mercy, rest, freedom, leadership, Mary, and so on. When
I do so, I consult a Bible concordance, which is an alphabetical index
of the principal words of the Bible with a reference to the passage in
which each occurs. I look up each passage and take notes, separate
the findings into categories, and draw conclusions. I have discovered
incredibly interesting insights this way.

When studying for exegesis to extract the information and
meaning from a passage, I consult the in-depth resources. I use
The Interpreter's Bible. I love my *Haydock Douay-Rheims Bible with
Catholic Commentary from the Fathers*. I use Bible study software
to study particular words in their original languages and to comb
through the Ante-Nicene and Nicene Fathers and the Catechism for
the passages I am studying to get the Church's historical voice. The
original languages offer rich insights. There is really no wrong way,
except to fail to begin.

So begin!

God is waiting to speak to us about our lives and loves and issues
and challenges every single day through the Scriptures. All we have
to do is read them with the knowledge and expectation that Christ,
the eternal Word of the living God, will open our minds through the
Holy Spirit to understand them (Luke 24:45).

> Now We, who by the help of God, and not without fruit, have
> by frequent Letters and exhortation endeavored to promote
> other branches of study which seemed capable of advancing
> the glory of God and contributing to the salvation of souls,

have for a long time cherished the desire to give an impulse to the noble science of Holy Scripture, and to impart to Scripture study a direction suitable to the needs of the present day. The solicitude of the Apostolic office naturally urges, and even compels us, not only to desire that this grand source of Catholic revelation should be made safely and abundantly accessible to the flock of Jesus Christ, but also not to suffer any attempt to defile or corrupt it, either on the part of those who impiously and openly assail the Scriptures, or of those who are led astray into fallacious and imprudent novelties. We are not ignorant, indeed, Venerable Brethren, that there are not a few Catholics, men of talent and learning, who do devote themselves with ardor to the defense of the sacred writings and to making them better known and understood. But whilst giving to these the commendation they deserve, We cannot but earnestly exhort others also, from whose skill and piety and learning we have a right to expect good results, to give themselves to the same most praiseworthy work. It is Our wish and fervent desire to see an increase in the number of the approved and persevering laborers in the cause of Holy Scripture; and more especially that those whom Divine Grace has called to Holy Orders, should, day-by-day, as their state demands, display greater diligence and industry in reading, meditating, and explaining it.[15]

Let's Review

This is how to study the Bible with the mind of the Church.

- *The Word of God is a person,* not a book.
- *I read and study the Bible in order to know Jesus,* and to know myself in him.
- *Divine revelation as the fullness of the deposit of faith consists of both sacred Scripture and Tradition.*

- *I cannot understand or interpret the Bible accurately apart from the historical Church.*
- *When reading and studying with the mind of the Church,* we consider the primary literal sense, then the spiritual, allegorical, and anagogical senses of Scripture.
- *In order to read and study with the mind of the Church,* I must use Catholic Bible translations and study resources.

INVITATION

"God, who spoke in the past, continues to converse with the Spouse of his beloved Son. And the Holy Spirit, through whom the living voice of the Gospel rings out in the Church—and through her in the world—leads believers to the full truth, and makes the Word of Christ dwell in them in all its richness" (*CCC,* 79). The eternal and perfect God—the Trinity—exists in a perfect and eternal relationship of love and creates humanity for the purpose of bringing individuals into that vibrant relationship. God made us so that we might participate in his life.

The ultimate goal of understanding God's revelation in Scripture goes hand in hand with the ultimate goal of exegesis (literary analysis): personal transformation and intimate union with our Lord Jesus Christ. As Blaise Pascal said, "Jesus Christ is the center of all things and the foundation for all things; he who does not know him knows nothing about the world and nothing about himself." We read and study the Bible to know God, and know ourselves more fully.

It was through my daily, disciplined, and sometimes boring lectio and study practice that God invited me to join him in his evangelization work, first in my own pitiful wounded soul, and then in the priceless souls of his people. Only God knows what treasures await you in the ancient words and delicate onion pages of the Bible. Deacon Harold and I can only promise that if you take up the habit as disciplined search for him, he will be found. Let's ponder that truth in our hearts in our last "God Prompt" together.

God Prompt—LOVE the Word

Lectio—Listen

> For I know the plans I have for you, says the Lord, plans for
> welfare and not for evil, to give you a future and a hope. Then
> you will call upon me and come and pray to me, and I will hear
> you. You will seek me and find me; when you seek me with all
> your heart, I will be found by you, says the Lord, and I will
> restore your fortunes and gather you from all the nations and
> all the places where I have driven you, says the Lord, and I will
> bring you back to the place from which I sent you into exile
> (Jeremiah 29:11–14).

Oratio—Observe

Perhaps more vividly than any other book of the Bible, the book
of Jeremiah reveals the inner struggles of a prophet of God. In his
confessions, therein he candidly relates his inner turmoil concerning
his purpose in a time when God's land was occupied by an enemy
nation and the people had given up the faith altogether. The inner
conflict between Jeremiah's loyalty to God and love for his own
people made his duty of calling them to repentance a constant
struggle, while he observed and experienced with them God's painful
judgment on their disobedience.

Is someone you love experiencing the painful consequences of
disobedience to God or abandonment of faith? Are you, by virtue of
the closeness of the relationship, also suffering? Do you feel a duty
to repent, or to call someone you love, also, to repentance and more
faithful obedience?

Reread the passage, above.

When God speaks *to* you, he is always speaking *about* you. What is
God saying to you through this passage?

Meditatio—Verbalize

Lord Jesus, I believe you are speaking about, and guiding my life and decisions through the Scriptures. I confess I sometimes have difficulties with some of what the Church teaches. But I desire to be in full communion with you, and my heart is full to overflowing with all I have learned in this book. Please help me as I embark on the adventure of my lifetime with you in the Bible on a daily, disciplined basis. Help me to trust all you reveal through the Church. As I read your word, please open my heart and mind to all you have to say to me, always, and every time. Amen.

Contemplatio—Entrust

Perhaps you want to imagine Jesus sitting beside you, keeping you company, looking at your heart's desire with admiration and respect.

Final Thoughts

Regular reading and Bible study is one of the most exciting adventures of our lives. The practice is infinitely worthwhile, even though, on many occasions, it can be dry and not particularly fun. Did you know there are plenary indulgences available for every half hour we spend in the Bible?[1] Jesus and the saints remind us that seeking God's face and will in the Scriptures is the deep well of their joy in understanding their purpose, especially in the midst of terrible suffering.

They show us single-minded devotion to understanding the message of the Bible and how their lives are found and come alive in it is the very lifeblood of their souls; it is what nourishes them to face difficulty and maintain trust in God's ultimate care for them. Such prayer pervades every aspect of their lives. Their lives become prayer.

Over time, the practices that command our greatest care eventually become the essence of our lives, and lectio and Bible study are no different. Jesus's life was a constant referral to the Scriptures. Jesus withdrew in important cases to be alone with the Father to determine how his ministry should come to fruition through the structure of those Scriptures that foretold him. Seeing God and ourselves in the Scriptures enables us, like Jesus, to make all of our lives prayer. But also like Jesus, we must make time for when we must be alone with God in the Bible.

Now that you have finished *Ignite*, can you explain why the Bible is considered the speech of God? What does that mean to you personally? What Scripture or idea that you encountered within it was most significant to you? In what specific area might God want to work in your life through this session on Tradition and the Word? Will you let him? How?

Let Us Pray

Come, Holy Spirit, fill the hearts of the faithful and enkindle in them the fire of your love. Send forth your Spirit, and they shall be created. And you shall renew the face of the earth.

notes

INTRODUCTION

1. St. Jerome, *Commentariorum in Isaiam libri* xviii, prologue. PL 24, 17B.

CHAPTER ONE

1. *Dei Verbum,* http://www.vatican.va/archive/hist_councils/ii_vatican_council/documents/vat-ii_const_19651118 _dei-verbum_en.html.

2. St. Jerome, *Commentariorum in Isaiam libri* xviii, prologue, PL 24, 17B.

3. There are two possible interpretations of this story, depending on how one reads the original text: Zacchaeus as extortionist scoundrel, and Zacchaeus as a very good Jew who is unfairly judged for his career choice. Since you may not have been schooled in Greek, we chose the interpretation most easily assumed from simply reading the text.

4. Adapted from Ken Gire, *Intimate Moments with the Savior* (Grand Rapids: Zondervan, 1989) 73–77.

CHAPTER TWO

1. You'll learn about concordances in chapter ten.

2. Catholic Encyclopedia, s.v. "Jehovah (Yahweh)," http://www.newadvent.org/cathen/08.

CHAPTER THREE

1. Pius XII, *Humanii Generis,* 36

2. *Dei Verbum,* 14–16.

3. Kirsten Weir, "20 Things You Didn't Know About...DNA," Discover Magazine, http://discovermagazine.com/2011/apr/20-things-you-didnt-know-about-dna.

4. Discover how the Holy Spirit is working through the patterns of your own toxic relationships, self-medicating habits, difficult circumstances, and over-whelming desires in Sonja's book, *Unleashed: How to Receive Everything the Holy Spirit Wants to Give You* (South Bend, IN: Ave Maria, 2015).

CHAPTER FOUR

1. The Torah, meaning Law, is the first five books of the Bible.

2. "Navel in Popular Culture," Wikipedia. https://en.wikipedia.org/wiki/Navel_in_popular_culture#cite_ref-136.

3. "Full Text of 'Hebraic Literature; Translations from The Talmud, Midrashim And Kabbala,'" Internet Archive, http://www.archive.org/stream/hebraicliteratur00harriala/hebraicliteratur00harriala_djvu.txt.

4. "People of the Land—Shepherdology: Understanding the Jewish Obsession with Shepherding." 2016. Chabad.org. Accessed July 6, 2016. http://www.chabad.org/library/article_cdo/aid/1762017/jewish/People-of-the-Land.htm.

CHAPTER FIVE

1. "Pentecost Definition and Meaning." 2016. Bible Study Tools. Accessed October 15, 2016. http://www.biblestudytools.com/dictionary/pentecost

2. St. Jerome, *Ad Tabiol,* 7.

3. Steven Todd Caster, "Zikkaron: Liturgical Remembrance and Sacred History." Term Paper, San Francisco State University, December 9, 1998. http://www.philvaz.com/apologetics/p39.htm, accessed July 30, 2016.

CHAPTER SEVEN

1. Cardinal Joseph Ratzinger, *The Spirit of the Liturgy* (San Francisco: Ignatius, 2000), 43.

2. "It is by the soul, enclosed within the body, that the body is held together, and similarly, it is by the Christians, detained in the world as in a prison, that the world is held together." From a Letter to Diognetus: The Christian in the World, http://www.vatican.va/spirit/documents/spirit_20010522_diogneto_en.html.

3. "Types, scriptural," in Fr. John Hardon, *Catholic Dictionary: An Abridged and Updated Edition of Modern Catholic Dictionary* (New York: Image, 2013), 550.

4. "ANF01. The Apostolic Fathers with Justin Martyr and Irenaeus—Christian Classics Ethereal Library," http://www.ccel.org/ccel/schaff/anf01.ix.vi.x

5. St. John Chrysostom, Catena Aurea, John 6:63, e-sword edition.

CHAPTER EIGHT

1. See chapter four of *Unleashed* for more information on predominant fault.

2. St. Irenaeus, *Against the Heresies,* book 1, chapter 10, no. 3

3. *Catholic Encyclopedia: Revised Edition,* ed. Rev. Peter M.J. Stravinskas, *Our Sunday Visitor* (Huntington, IN: 1991), 289.

4. Scott Hahn has probably written and spoken the most extensively on the covenant from a Catholic perspective. We suggest his books *A Father Who Keeps His Promises* and *Swear to God: The Promise and Power of the Sacraments.* The former is an overview of the development of covenant history, culminating in Christ and the Catholic Church. *Swear to God* is about the role of the seven sacraments as covenant oaths through which God fulfills his covenant promises.

5. DV 3–4

6. Theology of the Body.

CHAPTER NINE

1. The actual quote reads: "For there is made void in Christ not the Old Testament, but its veil: that so through Christ that may be understood, and, as it were, laid bare, which without Christ is obscure and covered." St. Augustine of Hippo, De Utilitate Credendi, §9, http://www.newadvent.org/fathers/1306.htm.

2. Jesus gives Peter the "keys of the kingdom of heaven." While most Protestants argue that the kingdom of heaven Jesus was talking about is the eternal state of glory, the kingdom of heaven Jesus is speaking of actually refers to the Church on earth. In using the term *keys,* Jesus was referencing Isaiah 22:22, which is the

only place in the Bible where keys are used in the context of a kingdom. In the old Davidic kingdom, there were royal ministers who conducted the liturgical worship and bound the people in teaching and doctrine. But there was also a Prime Minister or chief steward of the kingdom who held the keys. Jesus gives Peter these keys to his earthly kingdom, the Church. This representative has decision-making authority over the people—when he shuts a door, no one opens it. See also Job 12:14.

3. Jesus said in Aramaic, "You are Kepha and on this Kepha I will build my Church." In Aramaic, *kepha* means "a massive stone", and *evna* means "little pebble." Some non-Catholics argue that because the Greek word for a massive rock is *petra* and *petros* is the Greek word used for a small rock, Jesus was attempting to diminish Peter by calling him a small rock. However, using *petros* to translate *kepha* was done simply to reflect the masculine noun of Peter, as Jesus also renamed Simon "rock" in Mark 3:16 and John 1:42. To further demonstrate that Jesus was speaking Aramaic, Jesus says Simon "Bar-Jona." In Aramaic, *Bar* means "son," and *Jonah* means "John or dove" (Holy Spirit). Also, in citing "on this rock," the Scriptures use the Greek construction *tautee tee* which means on "this" rock, on "this same" rock, or on "this very" rock. *Tautee tee* is a demonstrative construction in Greek, pointing to Peter, the subject of the sentence (and not his confession of faith as some non-Catholics argue) as the very rock on which Jesus builds his Church. The demonstrative *tautee* generally refers to its closest antecedent *Petros*.

4. Cyprian of Carthage, AD 251. It is also important to note that it was only after Jesus established Peter as leader of the Church that he began to speak of his death and departure. This is because Jesus had now appointed his representative on Earth. Other illustrations of Peter's authority include: (a) John 21:15—Jesus asks Peter if he loves Jesus "more than these," referring to the other apostles. Jesus singles Peter out as the leader of the apostolic college; (b) Peter is the only apostle in the New Testament who Jesus speaks with alone; (c) John 21:15–17—Jesus selects Peter to be the chief shepherd of the apostles when he says to Peter, "feed my lambs," "tend my sheep," "feed my sheep." Peter will shepherd the Church as Jesus's representative; (d) Luke 22:31–32—Jesus also prays that Peter's faith may not fail and charges Peter to be the one to strengthen the other apostles—"Simon, Satan demanded to have you (plural, referring to all the apostles) to sift you (plural) like wheat, but I prayed for you (singular) that your (singular) faith may not fail, and when you (singular) have turned again, strengthen your brethren"; (e) Acts 1, 2, 3, 4, 5, 8, 15—no one questions Peter's authority to speak for the Church, declare anathemas, and resolve doctrinal debates. Peter is the rock on which the Church is built who feeds Jesus's sheep and whose faith will not fail; (f) Peter receives the first converts into the Church

(Acts 2:41); (g) Peter imposes the first ecclesiastical punishment (Acts 5:1); (h) Peter performs the first miracle (Acts 3:1); (i) Peter makes the first official ecclesiastical visit (Acts 9:32); and (j) it was Peter who, among the gathered apostles and presbyters, rendered the first dogmatic decision in the Church regarding whether circumcision is necessary for salvation (Acts 15:7).

5. *Lumen Gentium,* 21.

6. See *Lumen Gentium,* 22.

7. Ratzinger.

CHAPTER TEN

1. "Jesus Christ…completes the work of salvation which His Father gave Him to do (see John 5:36; John 17:4). To see Jesus is to see His Father (John 14:9). For this reason Jesus perfected revelation by fulfilling it through his whole work of making Himself present and manifesting Himself: through His words and deeds, His signs and wonders, but especially through His death and glorious resurrection from the dead and final sending of the Spirit of truth." *Dei Verbum,* 4. http://www.vatican.va/archive/hist_councils/ii_vatican_council/documents/vat-ii_const_19651118_dei-verbum_en.html.

2. DV 7.

3. DV 7.

4. DV 8, LG 12.

5. See also *CCC,* 94.

6. DV 1.

7. *CCC,* 116, quoting St. Thomas Aquinas, *STh* I, 1, 10, ad I.

8. Thomas Merton, *Praying the Psalms,* 7, 8, 11, 26, 9.

9. Teresa of Calcutta, quoted at www.acfp2000.com/Saint/Mother_Teresa/Mother_Teresa.html.

10. St. John Paul II, *Mulieris Dignitatem,* 18.

11. Sonja offers continuous topical Bible study series on her radio show, *Bible Study Evangelista.* Get her weekly shows adn LOVE the Word meditation at biblestudyevangelista.com.

12. I use the *New Jerusalem Bible* (NJB), the *Haydock Douay Rheims with Commentaries* (DRB), the *Revised Standard Version Catholic Edition* (RSV-CE), and the *New American Bible* (NAB), all ecclesiastically approved Catholic Bibles.

13. I use Fr. Hardon's and Dr. Scott Hahn's Catholic dictionaries. NAB and RSV-CE Catholic Bible concordances are available on Amazon.com. The Catholic Encyclopedia is available free at New Advent.org

14. See *Unleashed* for more in-depth information on spiritual pop quizzes.

15. Pope Leo XIII, *Providentissimus Deus,* 2.

FINAL THOUGHTS

1. *Enchiridion of Indulgences,* 50.

Ignite
DVD Series

Each 30-minute video in the *Ignite* DVD series offers you another opportunity to ignite your faith through the Scriptures with Deacon Harold and Sonja. Available at deaconharold.com

Episode 1: Intro
Episode 2: Purpose—The What of the Bible
Episode 3: Land—The Where of the Bible
Episode 4: Old Testament—The Who of the Old Testament
Episode 5: New Testament—The Who of the New Testament
Episode 6: Covenants—The Why of the Bible
Episode 7: Tabernacle 1—The How of the Old Testament, Part 1
Episode 8: Tabernacle 2—The How of the Old Testament, Part 2
Episode 9: Authority—Whose Voice Is His?
Episode 10: Last Things—Eschatology of the Bible
Episode 11: How Deacon Studies
Episode 12: How Sonja Studies
Episode 13: Lectio Divina—The Word Is a Person

About the Authors

Sonja Corbitt is the Bible Study Evangelista and creator of the LOVE the Word Bible study method. She's a Catholic Scripture teacher with a storyteller's gift—a Southern belle with a warrior's heart and a poet's pen. The author of *Unleashed*, *Fearless*, *Ignite*, and *Alive* (out 2018), Sonja's weekly radio show and other Bible study resources are created with you in mind—bites of spinach that taste like cake—to help you "love and lift all you've been given." Catch her newest study series on the *Bible Study Evangelista Show* where ever podcasts are offered. What's an "evangelista"? Find out at biblestudyevangelista.com.

Deacon Harold Burke-Sivers—known around the world as the "Dynamic Deacon"—is one of the most sought-after speakers in the Church today. He is a powerful and passionate evangelist and preacher, whose no-nonsense approach to living and proclaiming the Catholic faith is sure to challenge and inspire those who hear him. He holds a bachelor of arts in economics and business administration from the University of Notre Dame, and a master of theological studies degree from the University of Dallas. He cohosts "Living Stones" on Mater Dei Radio, and has appeared on numerous radio programs, including "Catholic Answers Live" and "Vocation Boom Radio." In addition, he is the host or co-host of several popular series on EWTN television. Deacon Harold is featured on the award-winning *Chosen* faith formation program and the author of the bestselling book, *Behold the Man: A Catholic Vision of Male Spirituality*.